AF261447

EGYPTIAN ART

Author: Elie Faure and Victoria Charles

Layout:
Baseline Co. Ltd,
District 3, Ho Chi Minh City
Vietnam

© 2020 Parkstone Press International, New York, USA
© 2020 Confidential Concepts, Worldwide, USA
© **Image-Bar** www.image-bar.com

ISBN: 978-1-68325-921-3

Printed in

Jean Capart, Elie Faure and Victoria Charles

EGYPTIAN ART

Eternal monuments, hieroglyphs, and the art of the Nile

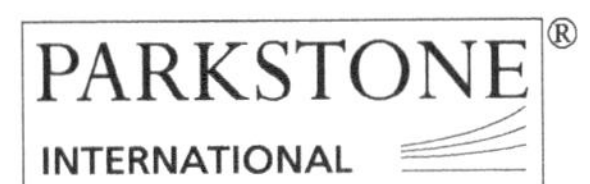

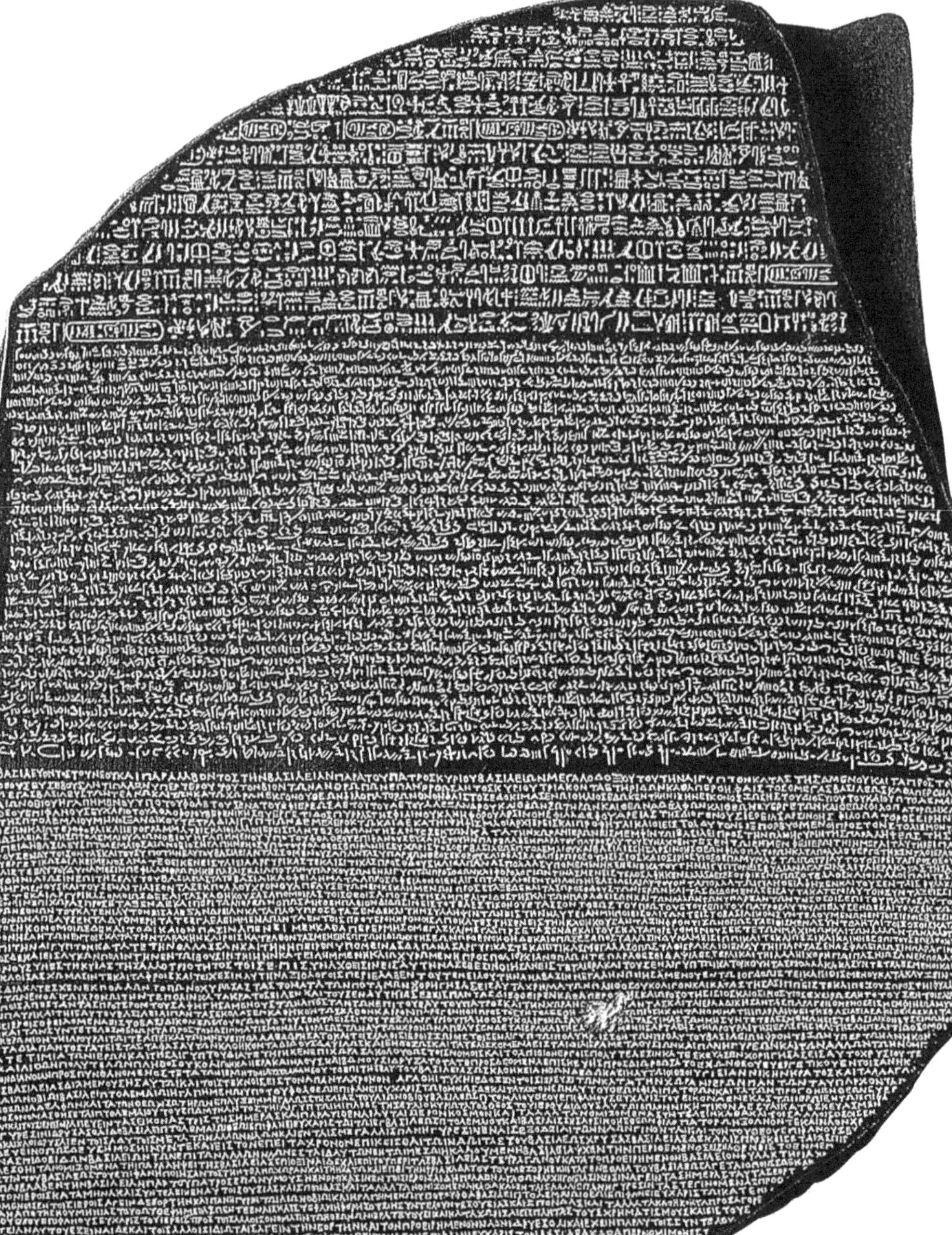

CONTENTS

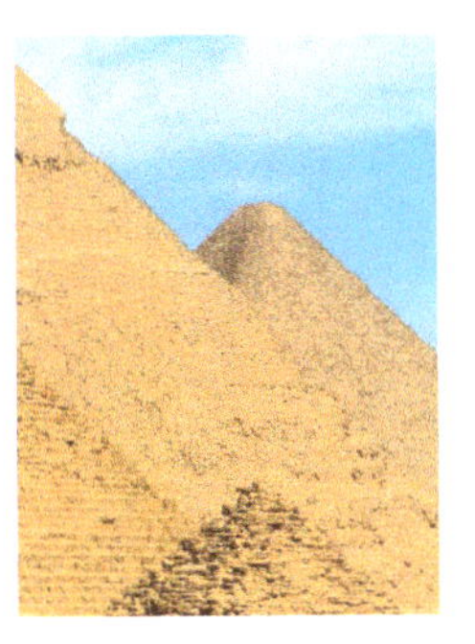

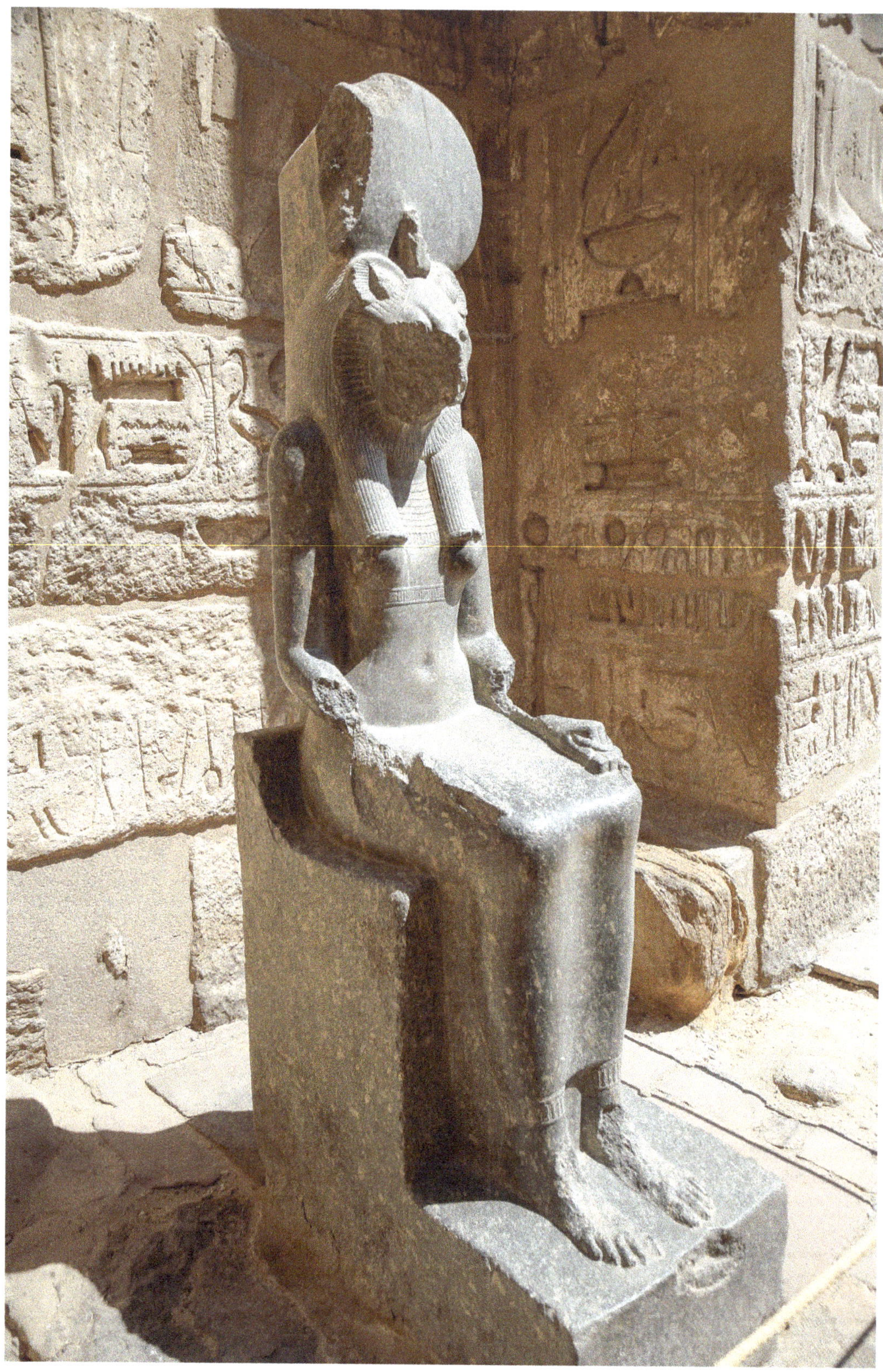

INTRODUCTION
THE COUNTRY: ITS CHARACTERISTIC ASPECTS

The natural introduction on Egyptian Art is a study, however summary, of the physical conditions of the country. Without exaggerating the influence of this medium upon artistic productions, it is nevertheless necessary to take into account the chief peculiarities of the Nile Valley, and to show in what respects this region essentially differs from almost every other land.

Let us glance at a map of Egypt. Across the great desert regions of northeastern Africa, the Nile forms a giant oasis, exceedingly elongated, which can be divided into two principal parts: the triangular estuary, called the Delta, and the course of the stream, which stretches far away toward the interior of Africa. The Delta is known as Lower Egypt, and the river proper, as far as the First Cataract, Upper Egypt.

Written in Greek and acient Egyptian, using three scripts (Greek, Egyptian hieroglyphs and demotic), the Rosetta Stone held the key to the decipherment of the ancient Egyptian texts.

Sculpture statue of landmark Egyptian warrior goddess Sekhmet also Solar deity and protector of pharaohs monument in Temple of Medinet Habu or Ramses III in Luxor Egypt Africa

Egypt is situated at the point of contact of three worlds: on its northern frontier it adjoins the eastern basin of the Mediterranean; on the eastern frontier of the Delta it touches Asia; and, by the course of the river, it effects a penetration into African regions. The natural frontiers of the north, the east and the west (Libyan or Sahara Desert) have never changed, but that of the south, on the contrary, has reached farther and farther up the course of the Nile just as the power of the kings of Egypt has extended to remoter regions. The First Cataract, in the Assouan District, constitutes the southern frontier of Egypt proper toward the south. The Pharaohs of the Ancient Empire rarely went beyond it: those of the Middle Empire conquered Lower Nubia; and later, Egyptian domination extended to Upper Nubia and even to the Sudan.

Let us first recall the brief and striking phrase by which Herodotus described Egypt as "a gift of the Nile." The time of the rise and of the ebb of its waters is so governed by the courses of the sun and the moon that there is one season of the year when all the elements of the universe come to pay to this King of Rivers the tribute

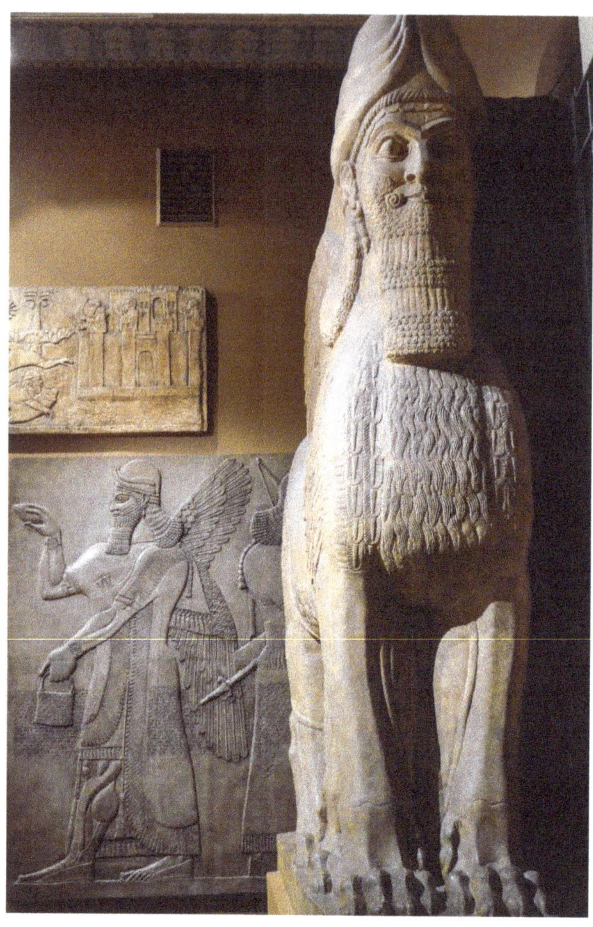

Moscow, Russia - Antique sculpture of sphinx and human murals in Egyptian room of Pushkin state museum of fine arts.

Historical artifacts in Egyptian Museum in Cairo.

Nile River of landmark Philae Temple ancient Egyptian public monument for the goddess Isis in Agilkia island Egypt Africa.

with which Providence has endowed them for his benefit. Then the waters increase, leave their bed and cover the whole face of Egypt in order to deposit there the fertile mud. There is no communication between village and village save by means of boats, which are as numerous as palm leaves. When at last the time comes when the waters cease to be necessary to the fertility of the soil, the docile river retreats within the banks which destiny has marked out for it, leaving the hidden treasures to be gathered. There are little copses of date palms, groups of acacias and sycomores, plots of barley or wheat, fields of beans or bersim here and there banks of sand which the slightest wind stirs up into clouds, and above all deep silence, scarcely broken by the cries of the birds or by the song of the oarsmen of a passing boat. The Nile unfolds its wandering course with the same motion amid the islets and its steep banks: village follows village at once smiling and dull beneath its canopy of leaves. «Every year, from June to October, the inundation drives the river from its bed: that part of the valley which is under water and on which the mud is deposited — the mud with which the water is charged — constitutes what might be called the real Egypt in opposition to the desert.

The Egyptians have bequeathed to us but scanty traces of their historical records. We know that from the earliest times they were wont to record important events in their history: indeed, there was even a special goddess relegated to preside over the annals of the Empire, but only a few fragments have come down to us.

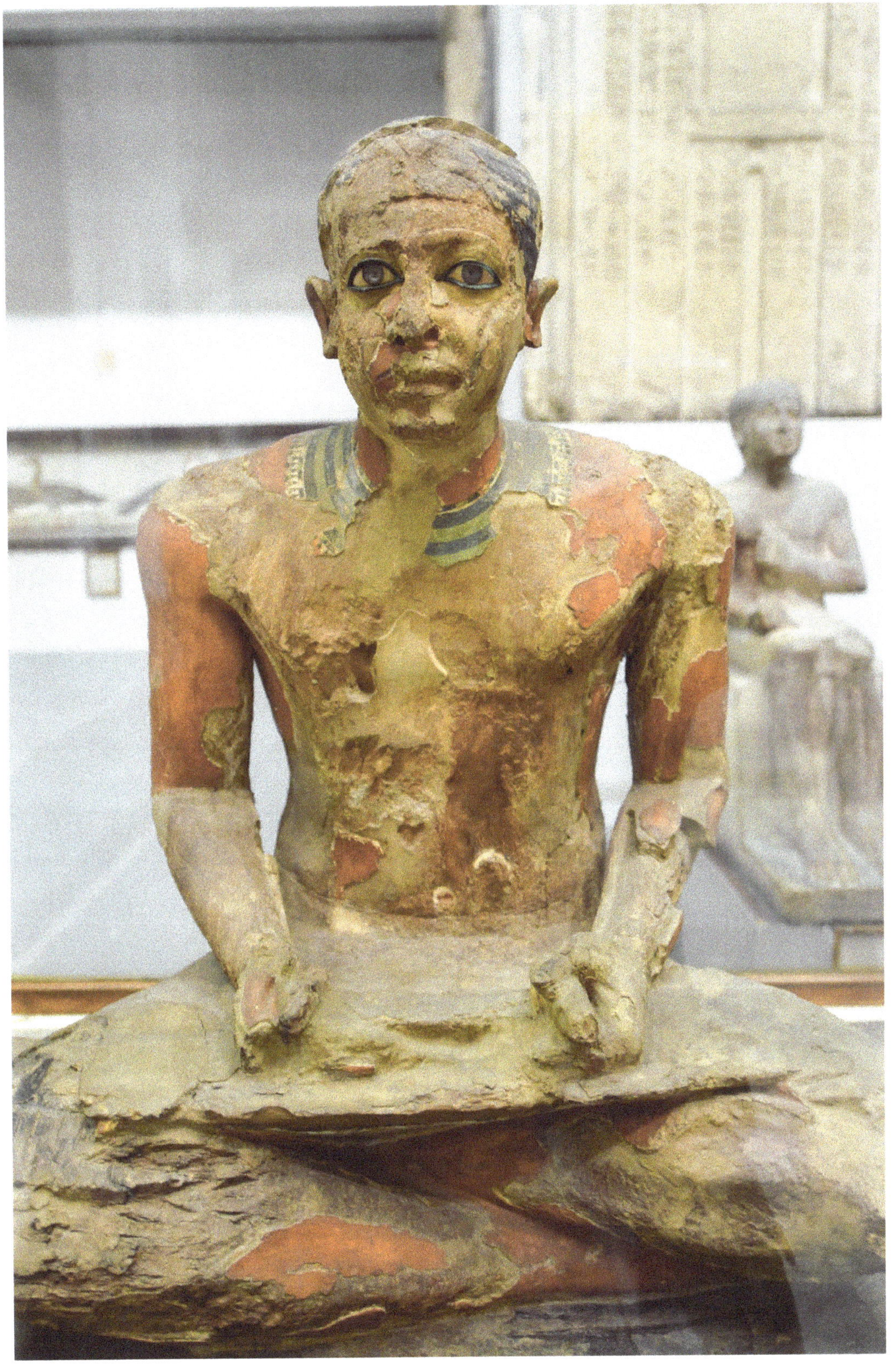

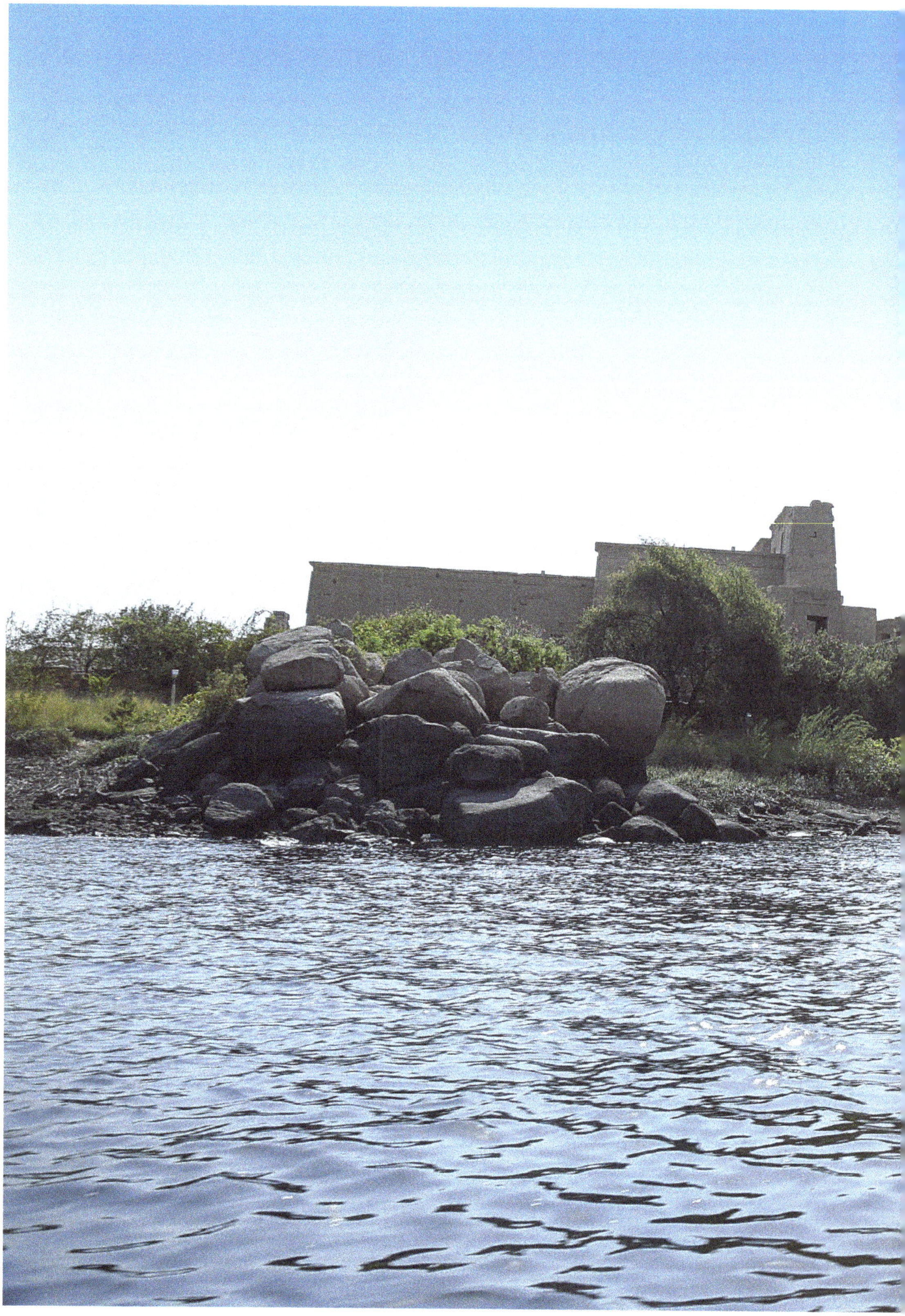

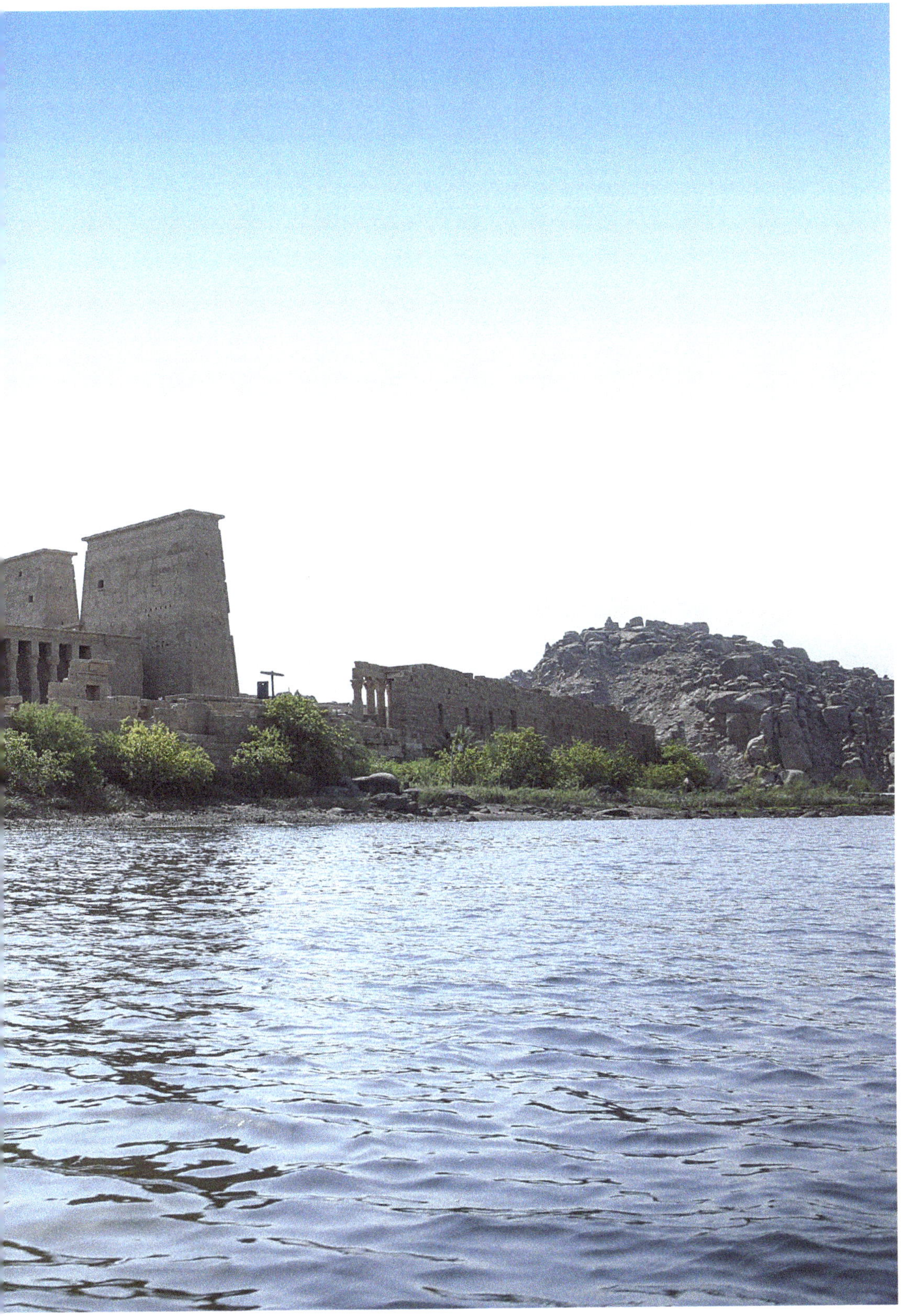

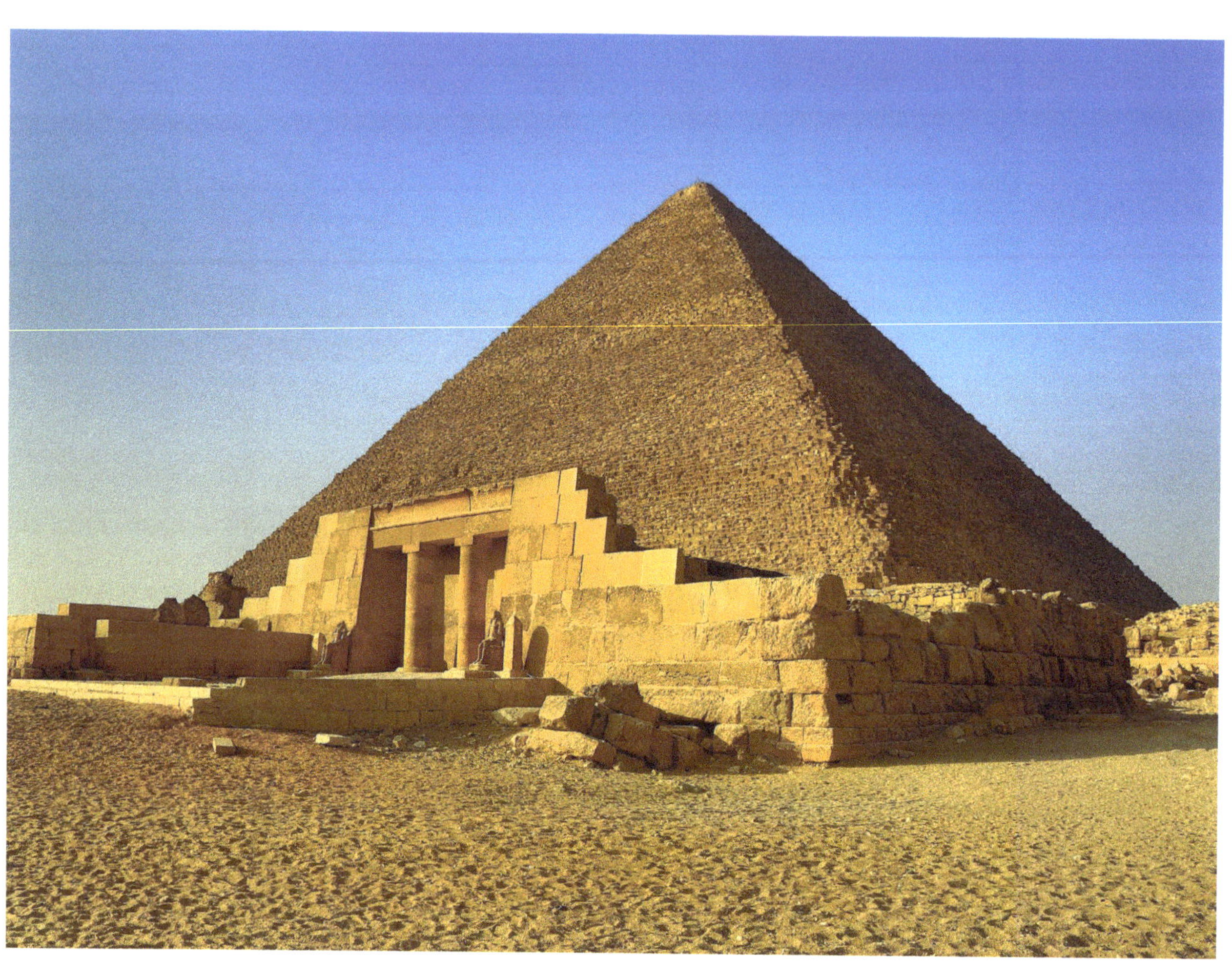

A GLANCE AT HISTORY

Can one compile, at the present day, a true history of Egypt, especially of the most ancient times? Information derived from the monuments, despite the great abundance of the latter, is, after all, of a very fortuitous nature. For one ancient papyrus which has been rescued, countless millions must have perished. ... It would seem that there still exists a great abundance of Egyptian documents, but they have to cover an enormous space of time. We can generally say that such and such a king carried out building operations upon such and such a temple; that he undertook a military expedition against such and such a neighboring country; that he returned with the spoils which he proudly enumerates; to which we may add a more or less lengthy catalogue of the monuments, which his contemporaries have left behind them. Our knowledge of the civilization of Egypt is much fuller, thanks to the biographical inscriptions and to the countless scenes depicted upon the temples and the tombs.

We must also allude to another important source of information, although the most difficult to use — the religious texts. These appear to us, from the times of the Ancient Empire, as the written version of a long and almost invariable oral tradition. They indicate to us a state of civilization which Egypt had long since left behind when these religious texts were used. The general impression which emerges from a scrutiny of these materials is that even the Egypt of the earliest dynasties had already a long past behind it.

The entrance of the mastaba of Seshemnufer IV and the Great Pyramid in background. Giza, Cairo, Egypt.

Ancient history is divided into the following division:

Early Dynastic Period	First + second Dynasty	I and I	c. 3150 – 2686 BCE
Old Kingdom	Third to sixth Dynasty	III, IV, V, VI	2686 – 2181 BCE
First Intermediate	Seventh to eleventh Dynasty	VII, VIII, IX, X, XI	2181 – 2061 BCE
Middle Kingdom	Late eleventh to fourteenth	XI, XII, XIII, XIV	1705 - 1690 BCE Second
Intermediate	Fifteenth to seventeenth	XV, XVI,XVII	1674 – 1535 BCE
New Kingdom	Eighteenth to Twentieth	XVIII, IXX, XX	1549 - 1077 BCE Third
Intermediate	Twenty-first to twenty-fifth	XXI, XXII, XXIII, XXIV, XXV	1069 – 653 B.C.E.
Late Period	Twenty-sixth to Thirty-fist	XXVI, XXVII, XXVIII, XXIX XXX, XXXI.	672 –332 B.C.E.

1st and 2nd Persian Period
Ptolemaic (Hellenistic) Period

From all this we perceive that there are two obscure epochs, one between the Ancient and Middle Empires, the other between the Middle and the New, and a confused period between the close of the New Empire and the 26th dynasty. We find that the first two of these obscure periods have been times of artistic decadence in Upper Egypt. With the inauguration of the Middle Empire (12th dynasty), of the New Empire (18th dynasty), and again under the Saite Empire (26th dynasty), the artistic traditions of the great epochs were successively revived. On each occasion, in fact, the models which served in the most brilliant periods of the Ancient Empire were reverted to, so that Egyptian art may thus be described not as a gradual artistic evolution which perfected itself as the ages rolled on, finally to deteriorate and die out, but rather as a series of deviations, or of decadence followed by renaissance. It is thus that we can explain the fundamental uniformity of Egyptian art, in a number of its manifestations, in spite of the great diversity which we notice.

Step pyramid in Sappara, Egypt.

View of pyramids from the Giza Plateau: three Queens' Pyramids the Pyramid of Menkaure the Pyramid of Khafre and the Great Pyramid of Giza (Khufu or Cheops).

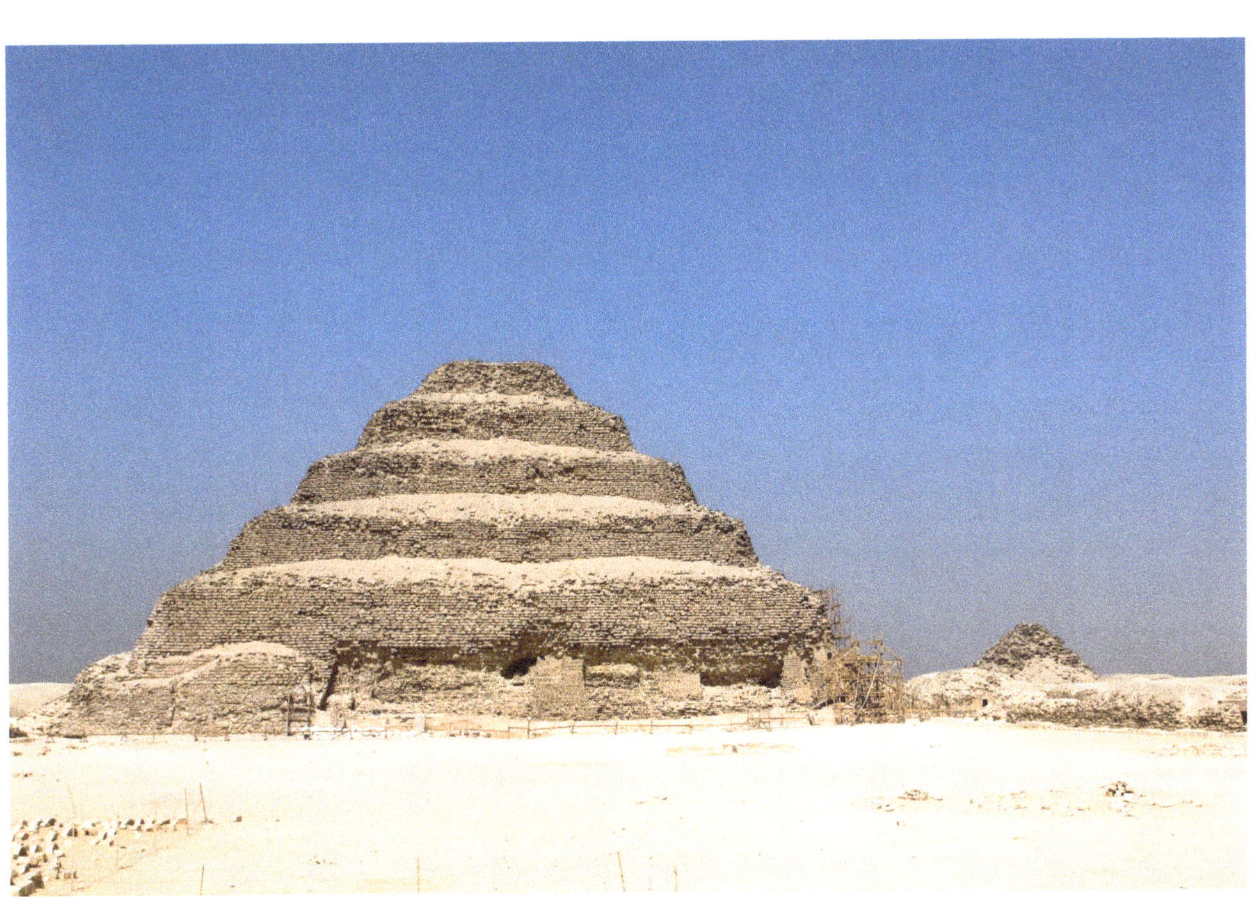

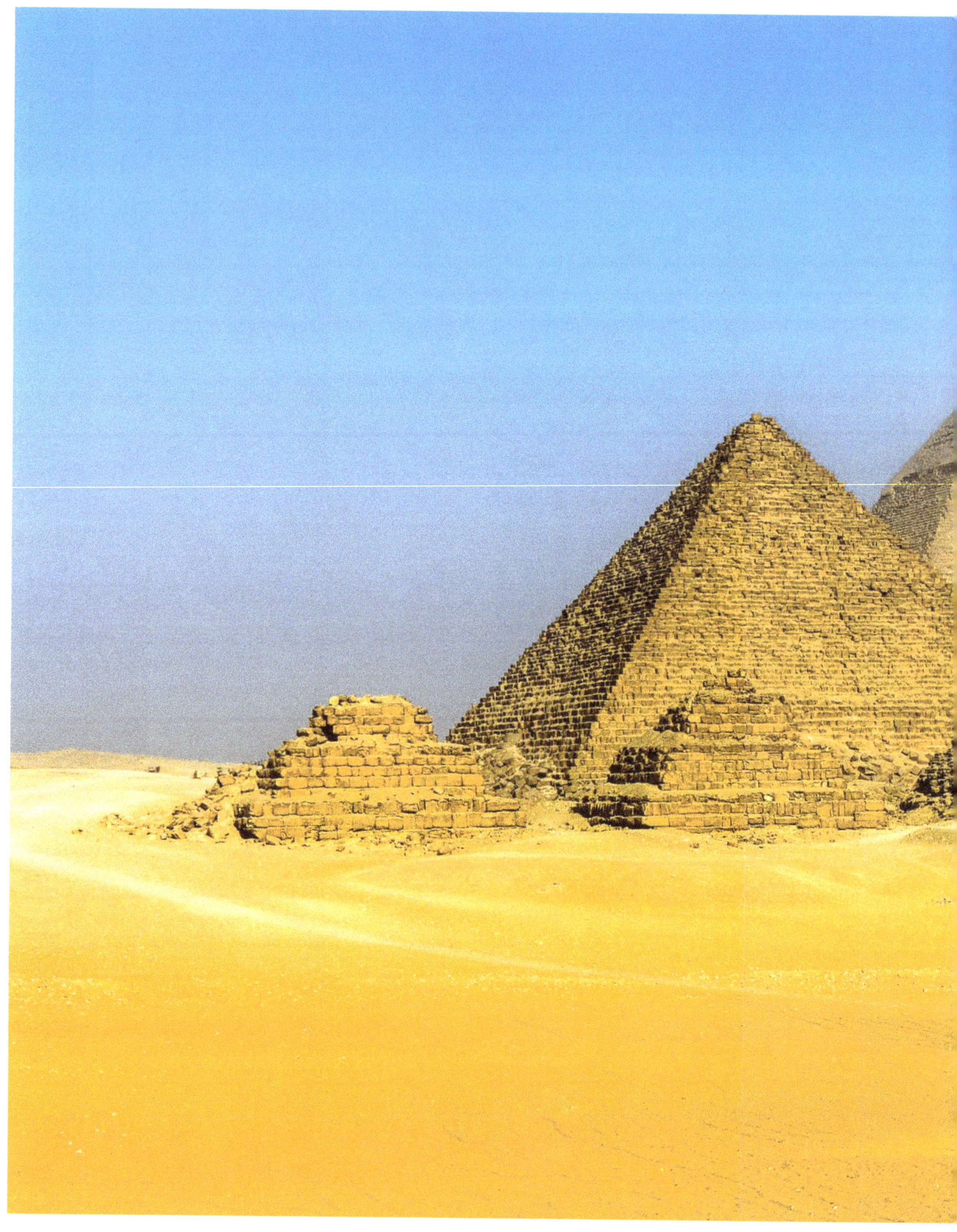

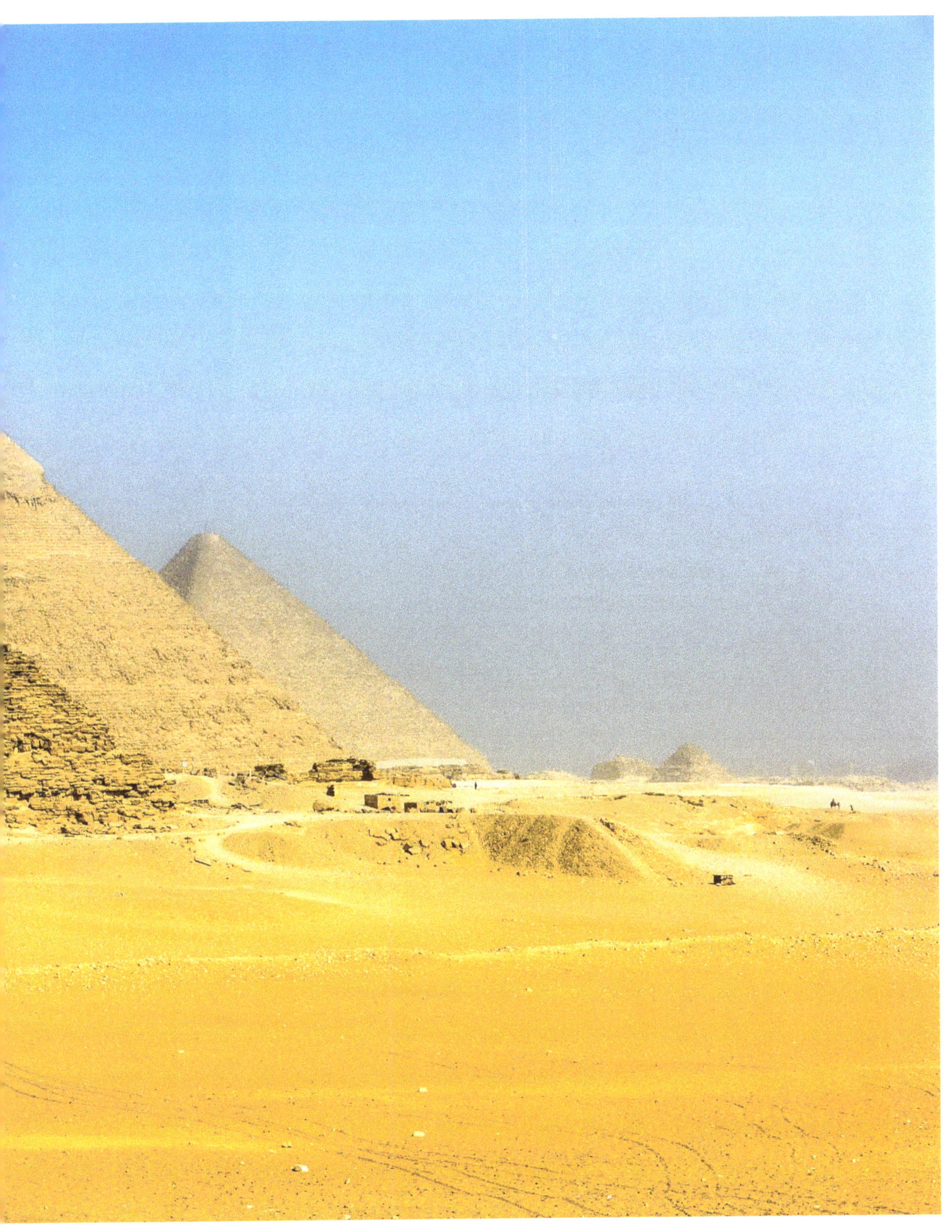

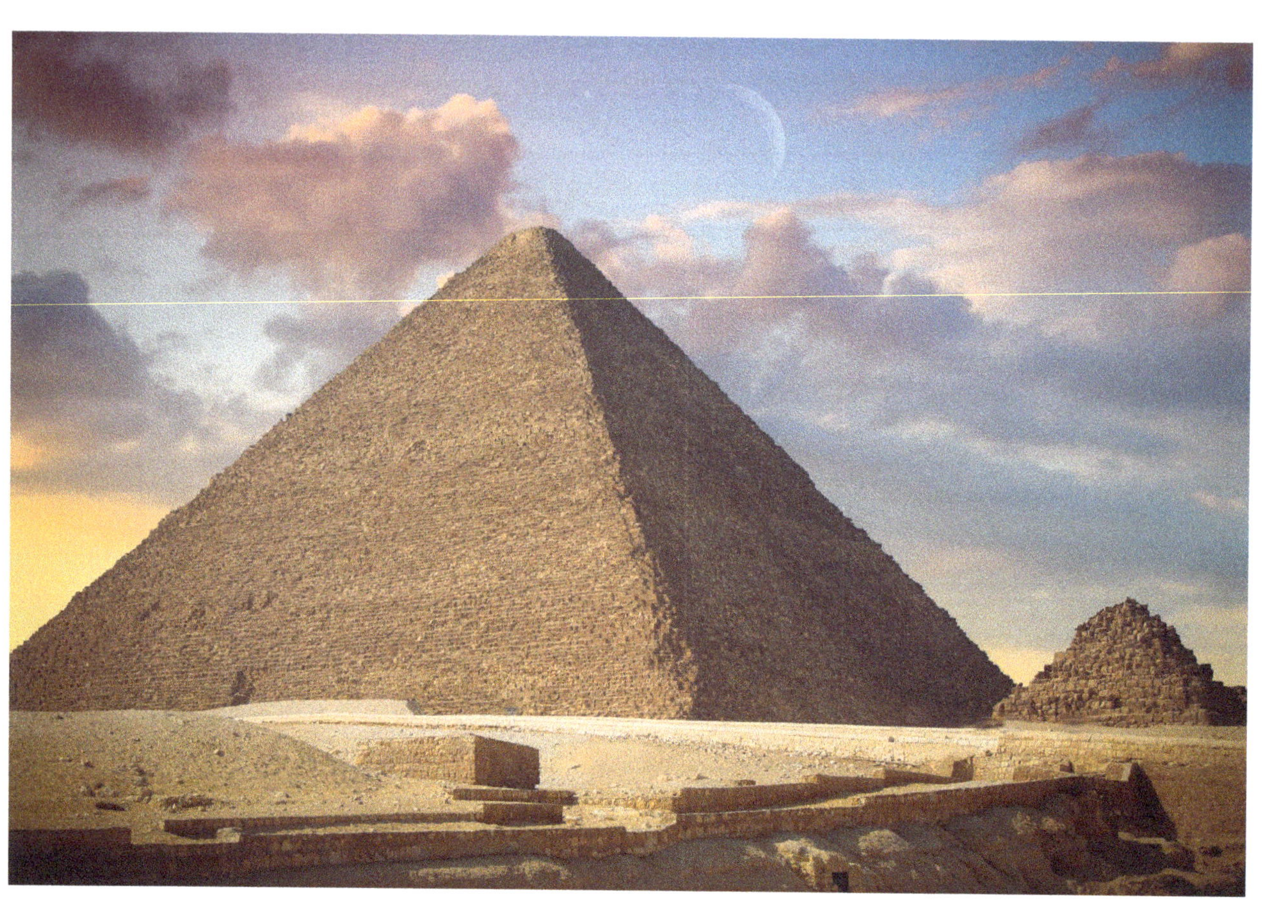

THE MONUMENTS

Let us try to form a general idea of the monuments which have come down to us. What has been said above on the subject of history in general cannot but be repeated in the case of the history of art. All our knowledge is above all things fortuitous; for certain periods materials abound whilst for others, on the contrary, there are none at all, although one cannot legitimately infer from this lack of evidence that the Egyptians had completely ceased, for long ages, to produce works of art.

Certain classes of objects have entirely vanished. It is sufficient to cite but one example: the decorative goldsmith's work, which is known to us through the representations of it on bas-reliefs and on paintings in the tombs and temples of the New Empire, where we see the kings presenting it as an offering to the gods, or the envoys of tributary states coming forward to lay it before the throne of the Pharaoh. Of another kind of monument, which is mentioned at times in the texts, it chances that a single

The great pyramids of Giza in Egypt.

specimen has survived. This is the great statue in metal of King Pepi I of the 6th dynasty.

The division of the country into Upper and Lower Egypt is an important one from the point of view of the preservation of works of art. One might say, almost without exaggeration, that in the Delta everything has disappeared, whilst in Upper Egypt, on the contrary, a great number of antiquities is preserved. This difference can be accounted for in various ways, of which we may cite a few instances.

In the Delta, on account of the great distance of the quarries, most of the buildings were necessarily constructed of wood or brick, stone being but sparingly used only in the principal parts, such as in facades or in doorways. The great growth of settlements and townships in Lower Egypt has led to a more and more systematic pillage of the ruins in order to carry off all the stones which can be re-used for building. The damp soil of the Delta has destroyed most of the objects confided to its care, whilst the desert of Upper Egypt has preserved them almost intact. But alike in Upper and Lower Egypt, other causes of destruction and disappearance are not lacking.

Even in quite recent times antique sites have been exploited as quarries: the temple of Amenophis III at Elephantine, for instance, which was an object of great admiration to the savants of Napoleon's expedition, was completely demolished a few years later. Travelers in the first half of the nineteenth century have described and published in their narratives of travel many once important ruins which have vanished completely today.

When one considers the countless wars and revolutions which have devastated the country (to say nothing of the fact that under the last dynasties Egypt submitted to at least two Ethiopian invasions, two Assyrian, and two Persian), and when one recalls the systematic destruction by the Christians who smashed the idols and the temples of false gods, and by the Arabs who mutilated all human figures, to say nothing of the ravages caused by excavators of long ago, one is astounded to find that so many Egyptian monuments still remain. And as though destruction by man were not sufficient, animals have done their share; one may instance the veritable invasions of white ants which have ravaged the ancient cemeteries.

It will now perhaps be convenient to draw up a kind of synopsis of typical groups of monuments, which must occupy our attention, picking out characteristic examples from each kind and for different periods. A monument of the 1st dynasty in the name of King Narmer (which some would identify with Menes, the first king to unite the two Egypts under one scepter) is known as the Palette of Narmer. It displays, among other things, a figure of the king clubbing a vanquished foe with his mace. From this monument onwards, the general association of ideas is fixed, and the same theme reappears again and again across the whole page of Egyptian history. The same palette, by its portrayal of a ritual festival, makes it possible for us to trace, from the very beginning, the complex of motives which originate in the art of this remote epoch. The stele of the Serpent King, now in the Louvre, is a masterpiece of execution. The falcon which surmounts the royal name is rendered with incomparable precision. One wonders for how long and with what thoroughness it must have been studied from nature before it became possible to seize with such perfection the characteristic form of the bird and to render the lines so simply and with so sure a hand that all the succeeding ages should find no need to alter in the smallest degree the outlines which thus became fixed and unchanging.

If we now glance at the reliefs on the wooden panels of Hesi, in the Cairo Museum, which date from the first part of the third dynasty, we shall find there, perfectly employed, the fundamental conventions in Egyptian drawing of the human figure. Thus, we see that the monuments of the first dynasties, rare as they are, display a fully developed art the execution of which is striking in its perfection.

The great necropolis areas, which extend all over the plateau of the Libyan desert from Gizeh to Meidum, have preserved an important series of architectural monuments; royal tombs, generally

The great pyramids of Giza.

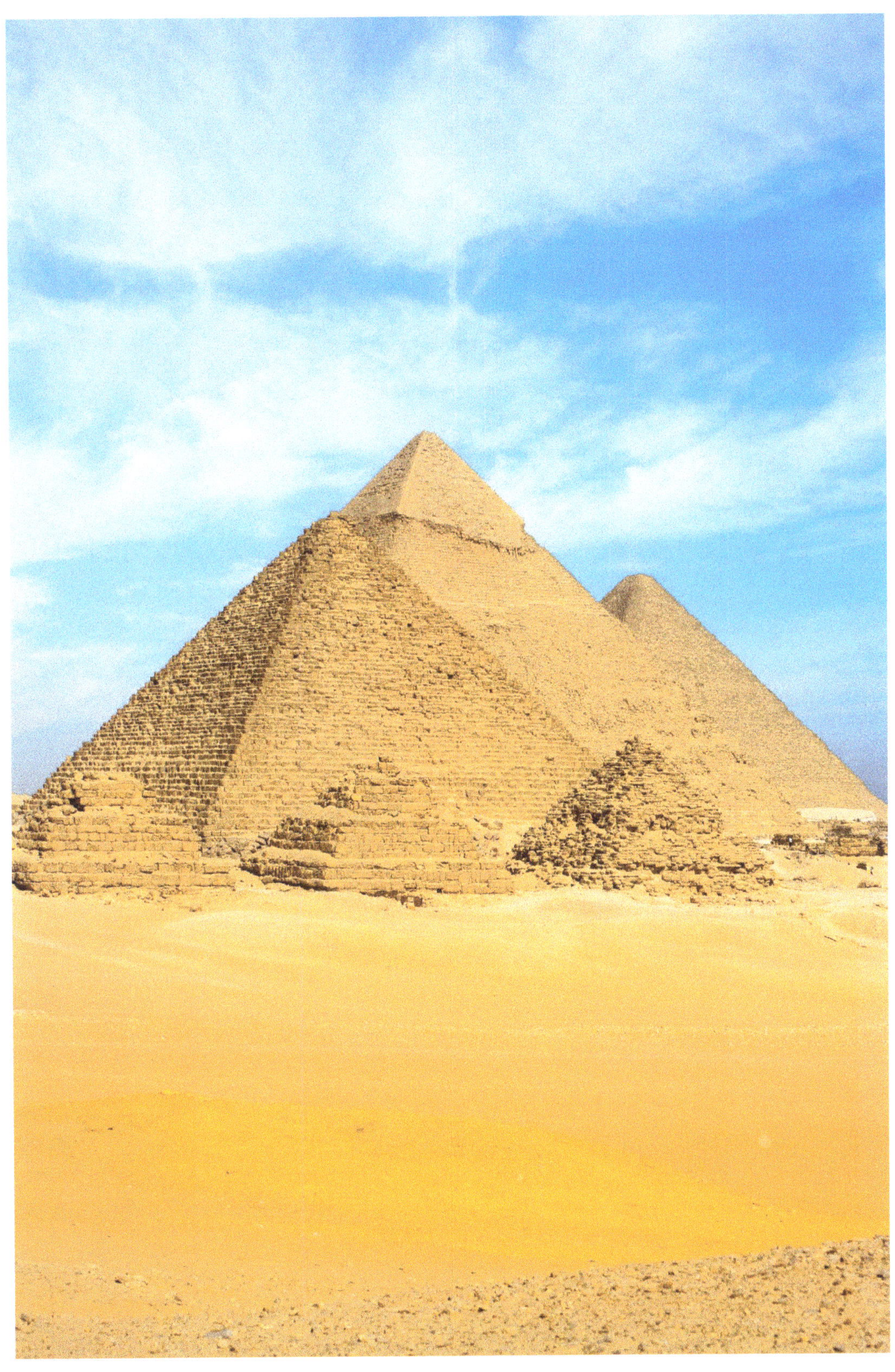

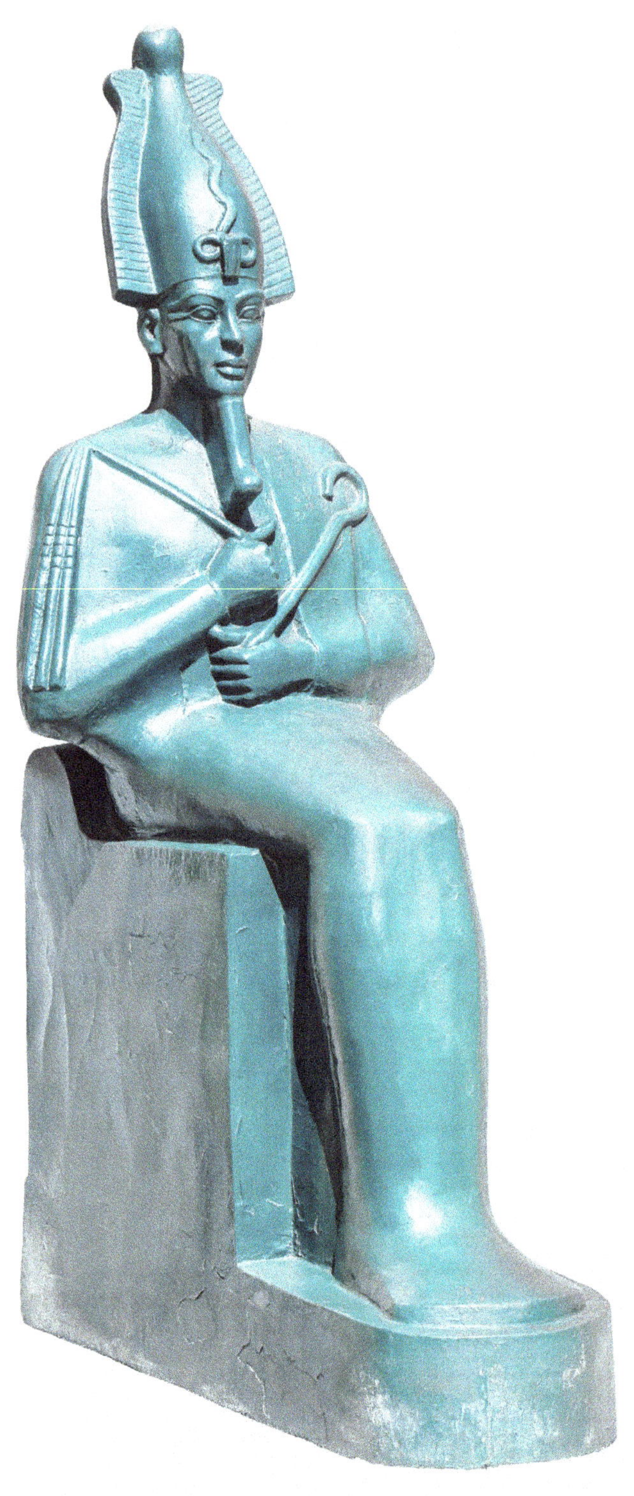
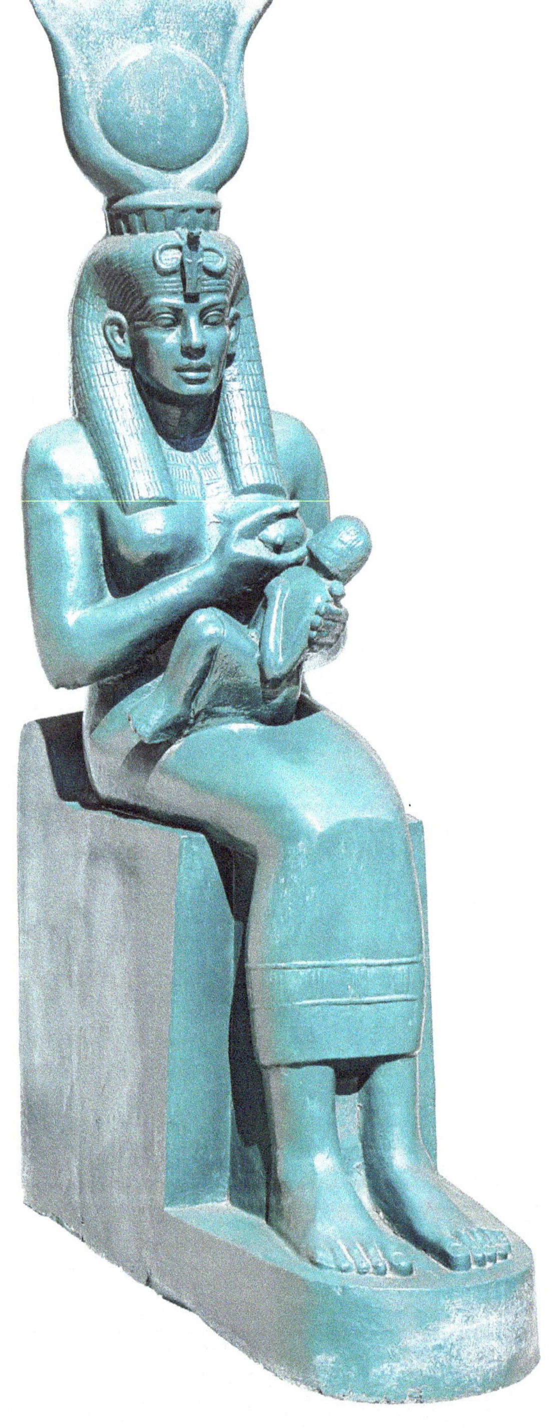

in the form of pyramids; funerary temples of the kings, adjoining the pyramids themselves; and the tombs of high officials of the type called by archaeologists, "mastabas."

To cite some instances: the reconstruction of the temple and pyramid of Khephren gives us a general view of the necropolis of Kheops and of Khephren. In the background the great masses of the pyramids tower above the burial chambers of the kings; on their eastern faces the funerary temples stand, connected by a long passage to a kind of vestibule in the valley, at the foot of the plateau. Numerous mastabas are grouped around the pyramids, or in the neighborhood of the vestibules in the valley below. The same general arrangement is met with around the pyramid temples of Abusir, where we shall find all the fundamental principles of Egyptian architecture in all ages employed by the architects of the 5th dynasty, especially the floral columns, which are the most typical elements of this architecture.

The mastabas, which are massive rectangular piles, appear too as architectural complexes containing in embryo all the fundamental parts of the sacred edifice of Egypt. The walls of the chambers within are covered with bas-reliefs and paintings; in niches or in recesses hidden in the masonry are found numerous statues which furnish material for the study of sculpture in the round. To name three examples: The first is a diorite mask in the Leipzig Museum, reproducing the features of Khephren.

Statue of ancient egypt deities Osiris and Isis with Horus isolated on white background

Detached from the statue, this fragment perhaps gains somewhat in beauty and lifelike intensity, separated as it is from the purely Egyptian peculiarities of form which sometimes offend our eye. Next comes the striking copper statue of Pepi I; it bears witness to a very advanced knowledge in the rendering of anatomical details. It is, in fact, a real masterpiece in metal work. The material of which it is made has permitted the sculptor to separate the arms and legs entirely from the trunk without having to make use of slots for fitting, which we find in stone statues. The two statues of Rahotep and Nofrit, found at Meidum, complete our examples of the perfection of Egyptian art under the Ancient Empire.

Later ages may perhaps have produced more elegant works, but they have never succeeded in surpassing the Ancient Empire in truth and in fidelity to nature.

All of a sudden everything seems to dwindle and disappear, and the few monuments of the intervening period between the Ancient and the New Empires are of such a kind as to provoke the belief that some irremediable catastrophe has occurred. The most casual glance at the Dendereh stele of the end of the Ancient Empire shows to what depths of ugliness and coarseness Egyptian art must have lapsed, at least in Upper Egypt. Had we not precise information as to date, one might easily imagine that the Dendereh reliefs are centuries older than the admirable statues of the Ancient Empire. One can scarcely attribute this to the clumsiness of some inexperienced craftsman, of whom a poor man had requisitioned a funerary stele in some provincial town. The royal monuments of the 11th dynasty give a scarcely better impression, for we find the fragments of a certain King Mentuhotep at Gebelein, reproducing the theme of the Narmer palette, which is treated in a stiff and angular fashion without any life.

But a very short time had to pass before the kings of the 12th dynasty had completely revived the traditions of the Ancient Empire. The bas-reliefs of Sesostris I at Koptos, as well as at Karnak, show us once more in their conception and execution the perfection of the work of the Ancient Empire.

We know of few great architectural monuments of the Middle Empire. Plenty of temples had fallen into ruin in the course of ages, had been restored, rebuilt or enlarged by the sovereigns of the New Empire. A study, however, of the great funerary temple of the 11th dynasty at Deir-el-Bahari, whose ruins give us the data necessary for such a reconstruction, will serve to give a good idea of the abilities of their architects. A careful study should be made of a number of interesting documents of the Middle Empire: the tombs of the nomarchs or provincial governors in Upper Egypt, the most remarkable of which are at Beni Hasan. The façade of the tomb of Chnumhotep II is justly celebrated for its so-called proto-Doric columns, and displays a standard of beauty and simplicity which only the architects of Greece, who came centuries later, were able to surpass. The walls of these same tombs present a most interesting series of reliefs and paintings. Two lucky " finds " of caskets containing royal jewelry at Dahshur and at Illahun make a welcome contribution to the study of the industrial arts.

The New Empire will testify to a fresh revival of all the ancient traditions, when architecture will flourish on a majestic scale in the temples of the gods and of the funerary cult Thebes and Abydos, to name but the two most important sites, will furnish us with ample material for study. It will suffice here to cite one or two instances: the colonnade, in classic style, of the great temple of Queen Hatshepsut at Deir-el-Bahari is certainly one of the most amazing works, which Egyptian architecture has bequeathed to us. Only the Cavetto cornice which surmounts the entablature informs us that we are not in the presence of a creation of the classic architects; but the bas-reliefs and the inscriptions stand there as an irrefutable proof against any classic influence, and show that the builders of Deir-el-Bahari lived a thousand years before the childhood of Greek architecture.

Luxor is a well-known name in the history of art: it is there that stand the gigantic piles to which the greatest kings of the 18th and 19th dynasties devoted their building activities. But it is at Karnak that the taste for the colossal manifests itself in all its fulness. The hypostyle hall, so vast that it could contain the whole of the structure of the cathedral of Notre Dame at Paris, has its roof upheld by 134 columns, of which the highest are as massive as the Vendome Column.

Nefertari, the favourite wife of Ramesses II, is introduced to various deities in scenes from the vestibule of her tomb in the Valley of the Queens.

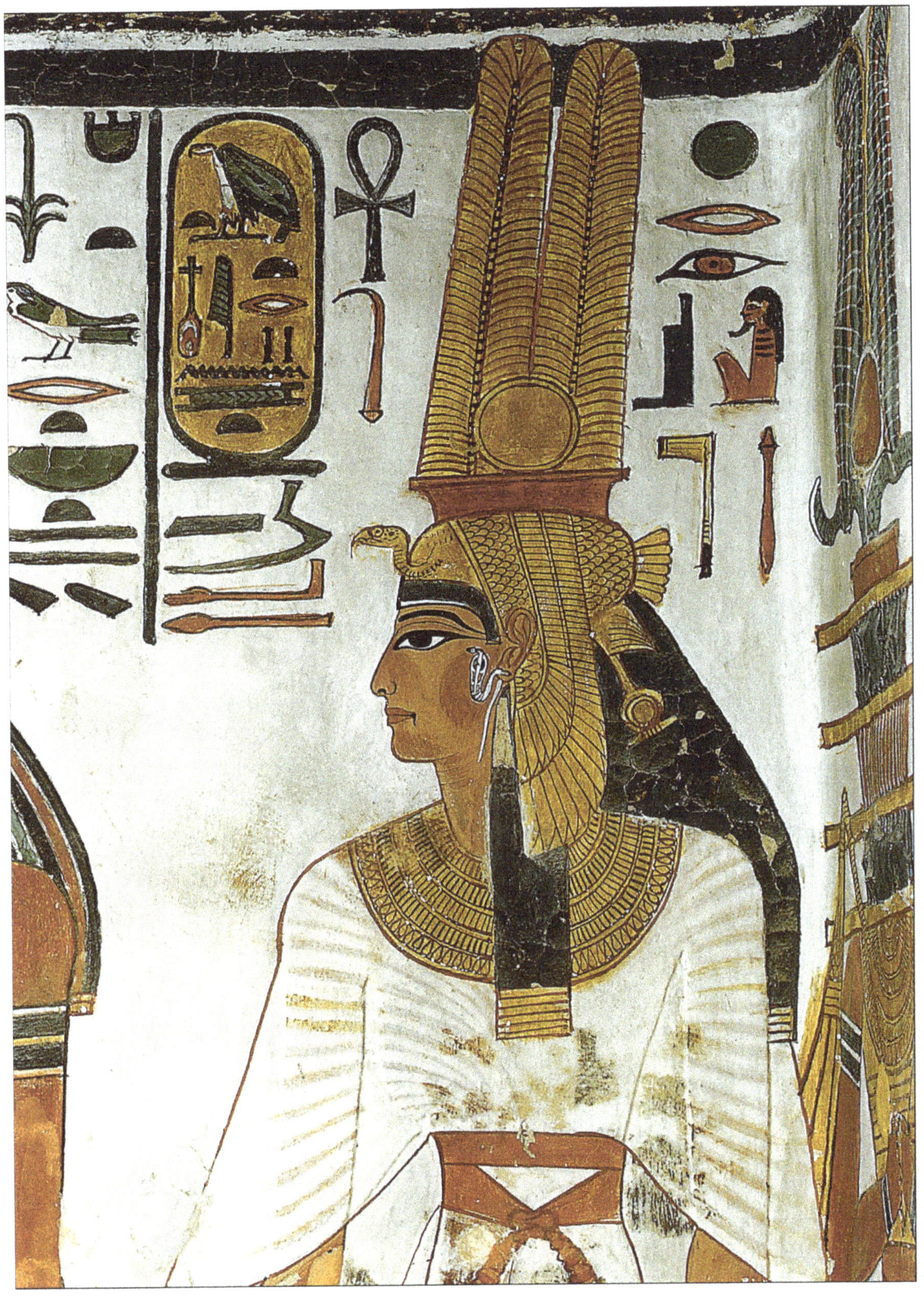

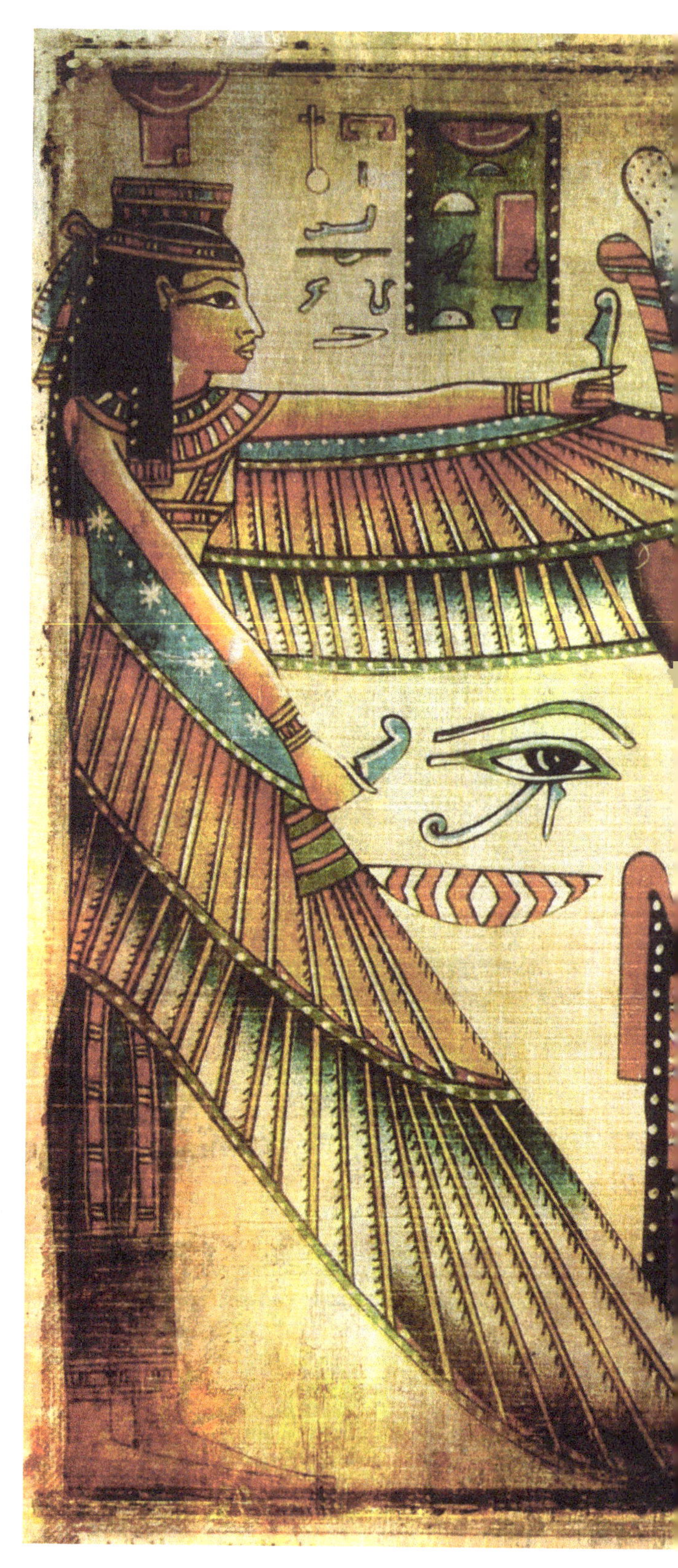

Ancient Egyptian papyrus.

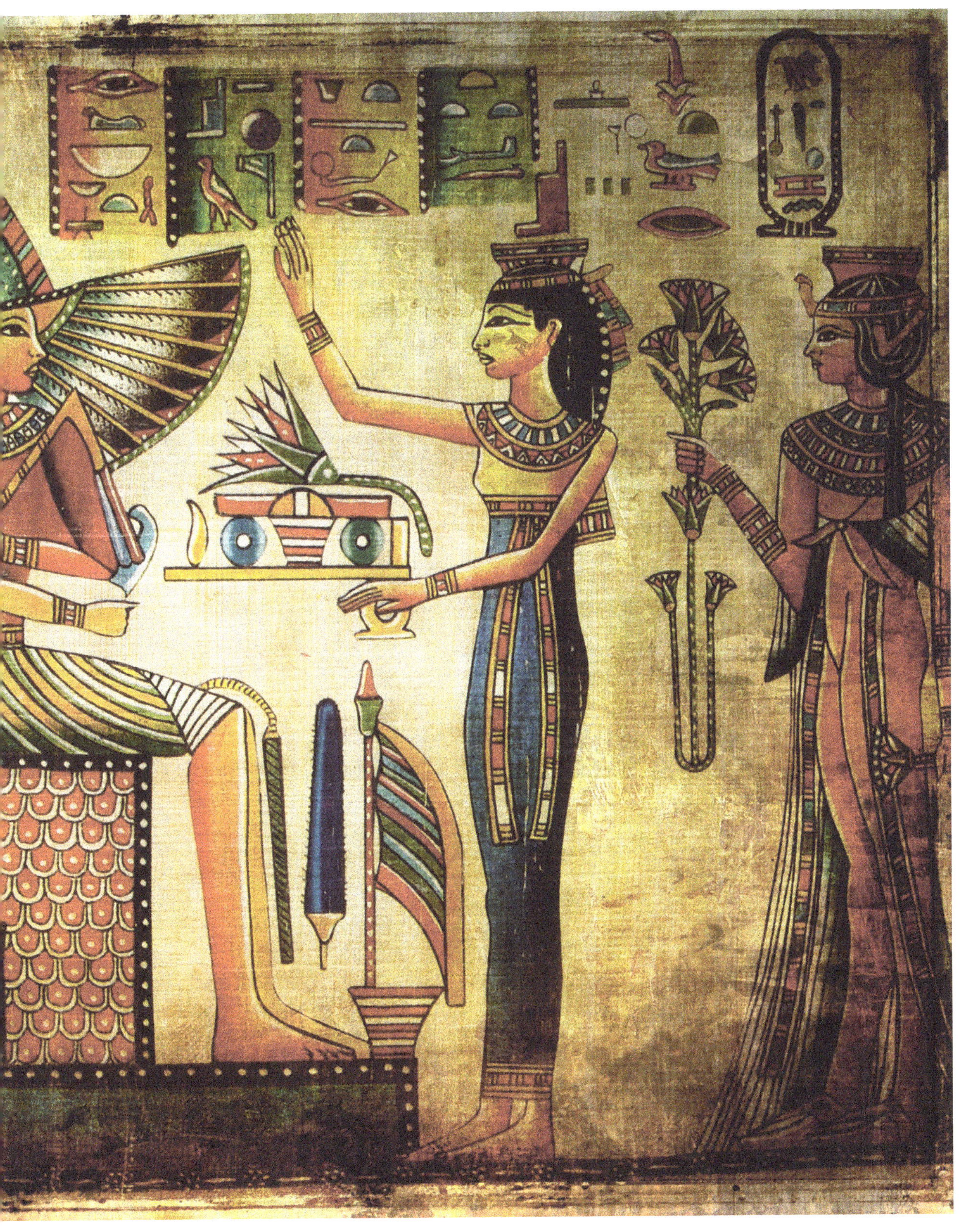

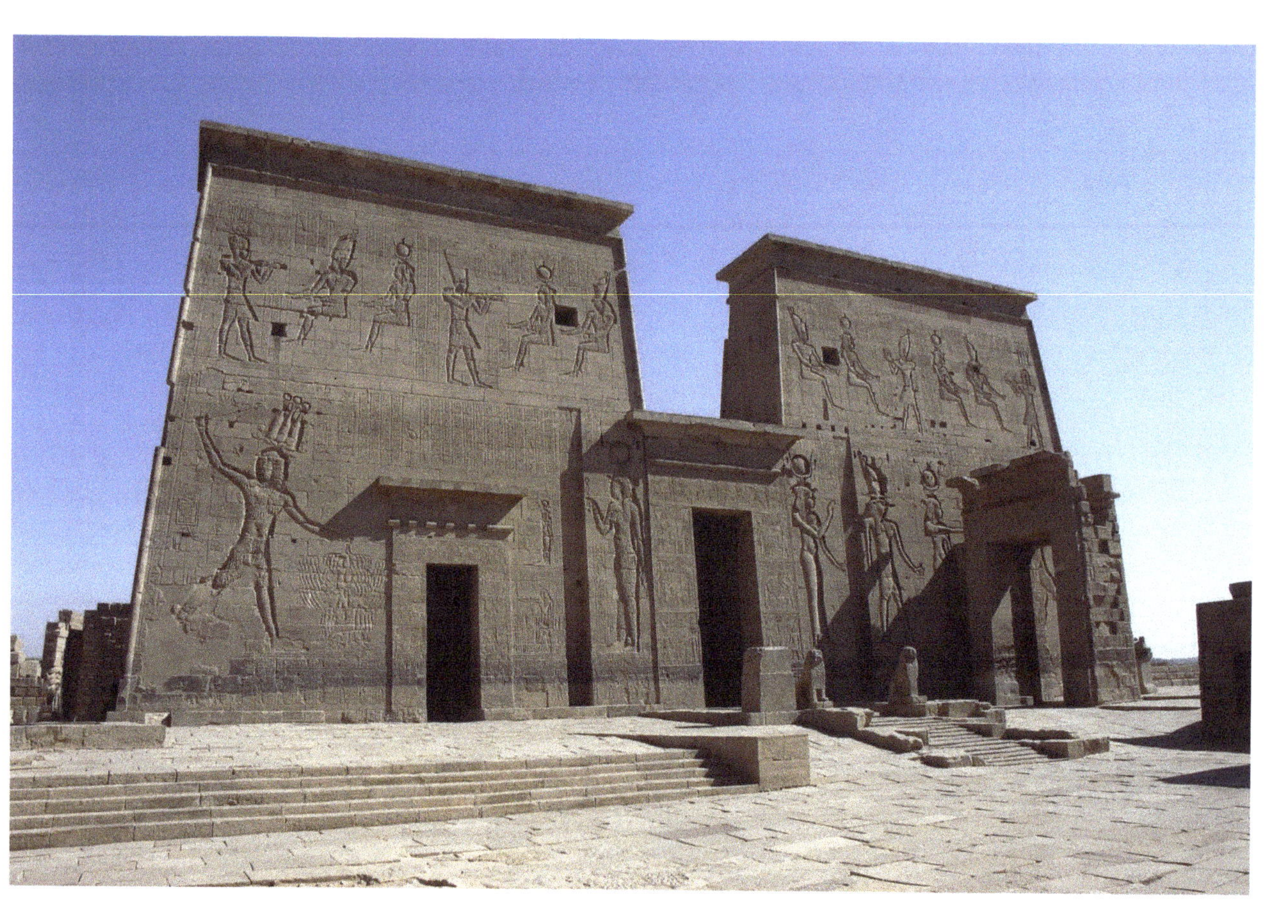

TUTANKHAMUN, PHARAOH OF THE EIGHTEENTH DYNASTY

Tutankhamun was a pharaoh of the Eighteenth Dynasty (c. 1332–1323 BCE) during the period known as the New Kingdom. His tomb nestled in the desolate Valley of the Kings on the west bank of the Nile just opposite Luxor was discovered in 1922 by Howard Carter. It was the richest royal tomb of antiquity ever found.

The ancient monuments of Egypt testify that the early Egyptians prepared for death as thoroughly as for life. Eternity was emphasized and, possibly as a consequence of this belief and the way it was carried out, the names of the Pharaohs have endured for more than three millennia. The Egyptians believed that the soul, living on after death, needed a home. Each tomb therefore contained the many possessions one might need for a future life - including murals, decorative arts and jewelry - and even servants, who could do the King's work in the afterworld, in the form of Shawabty figures.

Tutankhamun's tomb was crammed with magnificent furniture, statuary and countless glistening objects of gold. A coffin of massive gold held the mummified body of Tutankhamun, Canopic receptacles were used to preserve the young Pharaoh's viscera and an alabaster lid from one of them, in the form of the King's head, is in the exhibition. Also in the exhibition are: a miniature gold coffin in the likeness of the King; a turquoise-colored glass and gold headrest; a ceremonial flail and crook of gold and blue glass - both symbols of the Pharaoh power; the King's favorite hunting knife fashioned of gold and found enclosed in the mummy's linen wrappings; the young monarch's gold walking stick embellished with a figure in his likeness; libation jars decorated chests; statuettes of gods; pectorals; rings; amulets and scarabs. The scarab was one of the many protective amulets placed on the mummy. The Egyptians believed that the scarab had the power to bring about the resurrection of the dead.

Ancient Temple of Philae in Egypt by the Nile River.

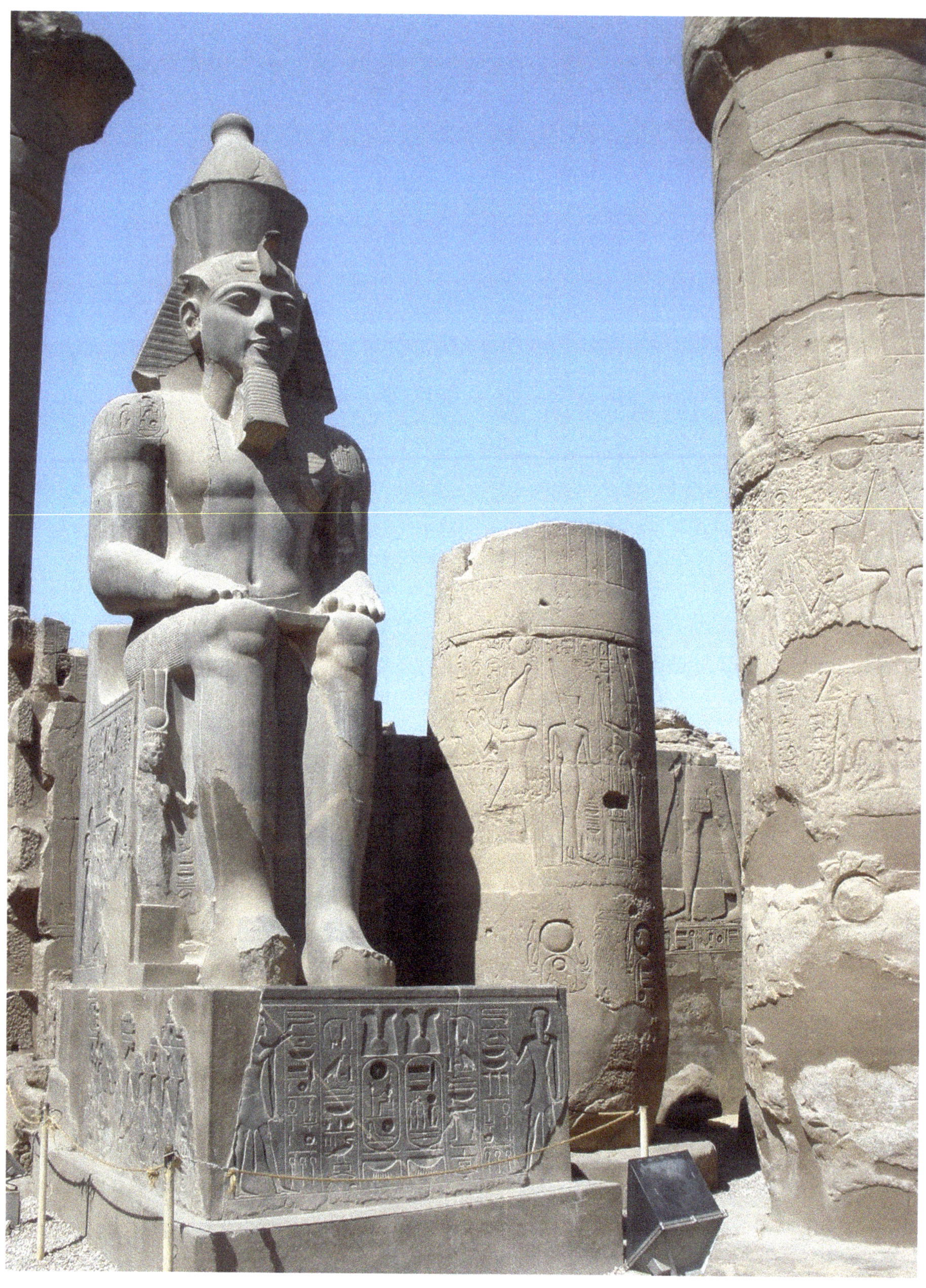

AKHENATEN, PHARAOH OF THE EIGHTEENTH DYNASTY.

Akhenaten meaning ("living spirit of Aten") (1353–1336 BCE) known before the fifth year of his reign as Amenhotep IV (sometimes given its Greek form, Amenophis IV, meaning Amun is satisfied), was a Pharaoh of the midst of the Eighteenth Dynasty of Egypt who ruled for 17 years. He is especially remembered for his attempt at a religious conversion of ancient Egypt, abandoning traditional Egyptian polytheism and introducing worship centered on the Aten cult, which is sometimes described as monotheistic. Aten, the sun disc, became the center of Egypt's religious life, leading to the complete elimination of the names of Amun, a pre-eminent Egyptian god, from monuments and documents throughout Egypt's empire.

We must assign a special place to the monuments which are associated with the name of Akhenaten. This strange Pharaoh, the religious and political reformer, has set his mark upon all the artistic productions of his time. The merest glance at the most exquisite piece of the series, the head of the queen in Berlin Museum, reveals to the beholder an aspect of Egyptian art widely different from everything else connected with the ordinary acceptance of the term.

His reign is known as the Amarna Period because he moved the capital of Egypt from the traditional site at Thebes to Akhetaten that he founded (in English transliteration Akhetaten means "Horizon of the Aten)". The city, which was abandoned shortly after his death, came to be known as Amarna. After his death, traditional religious practice was gradually restored, and when some dozen years later, rulers without clear rights of succession from the Eighteenth Dynasty founded a new dynasty, they discredited Akhenaten and his immediate successors, referring to Akhenaten himself as "the enemy" in archival records.

Luxor Temple is a large Ancient Egyptian temple complex located on the east bank of the Nile River in the city today known as Luxor (ancient Thebes) and was founded in 1400 BCE.

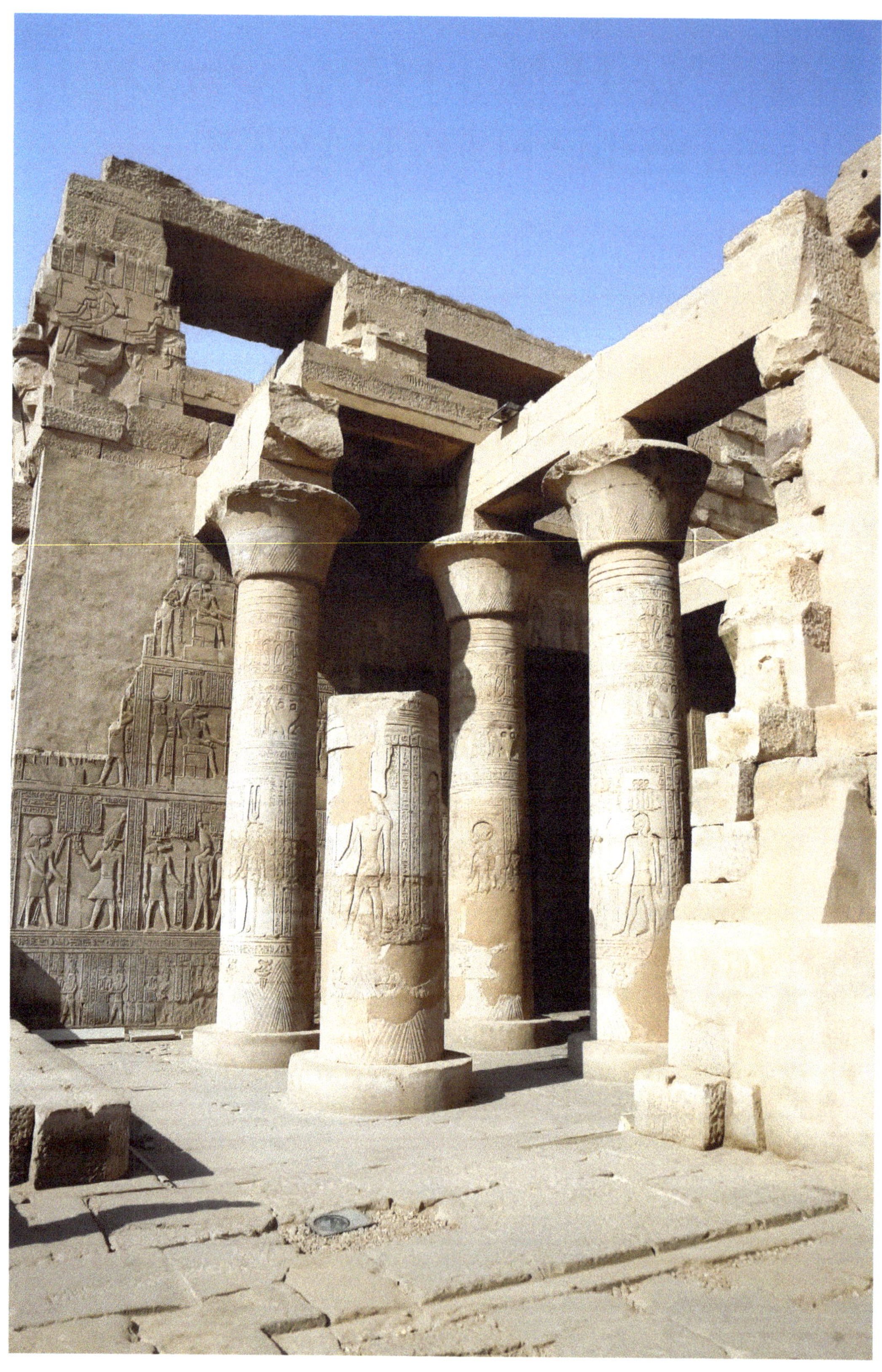

NEFERTITI, QUEEN OF THE EIGHTEENTH DYNASTY

Nefertiti (c. 1370 – c. 1330 BCE) whose name means "a beautiful woman has come," was a queen of Egypt and the wife of King Akhenaten. She ruled alongside Akhenaten during the Eighteenth Dynasty. She enjoyed an unusual status for a queen. Early artistic representations of her tend to be indistinguishable from her husband's except by her regalia, but soon after the move to the new capital, Nefertiti begins to be depicted with features specific to her. Why Akhenaten had himself represented in the bizarre, strikingly androgynous way he did, remains a vigorously debated question.

As Amenhotep IV, Akhenaten was married to Nefertiti at the very beginning of his reign, and six daughters, but no sons were identified from inscriptions. Recent DNA analysis has revealed he also fathered Tutankhaten with his biological

Landmark ruins Temple of Kom Ombo Egyptian monument from 180 to 47 B.C. in Ptolemaic dynasty with columns reliefs carving images and hieroglyphs in Aswan Egypt Africa.

The temple of Abu Simbel in Egypt.

sister. From the earliest years of the heretic king Akhenaten's reign, Nefertiti was distinctive because of her prominence in representations of cult scenes. Her participation in the rituals of the new religion was equal to that of her husband. In some parts of the Karnak temples of the Aten, the figure of the queen actually dominates the decoration.

Akenaten seems to have had a great love for his Chief Royal wife. They were inseparable in early reliefs, many of which showed their family in loving compositions. In some portrayals Nefertiti is only distinguishable from Akhenaten by their crowns and cartouches. This may reflect that they were siblings or related. The famous bust found in Amarna in 1912 shows not only her great beauty, but also a woman of strength and vision, capable of starting her own cult, and of ruling.

Ludwig Borchardt, a German archaeologist, and his team unearthed an exquisite limestone bust of Nefertiti, sculpted by Thutmose in c. 1360 BCE. The bust is 48 centimeters tall, weighs about 20 kilograms and is housed in the Neues Museum in Berlin. Its companion piece, a bust of Akhenaten, had been smashed.

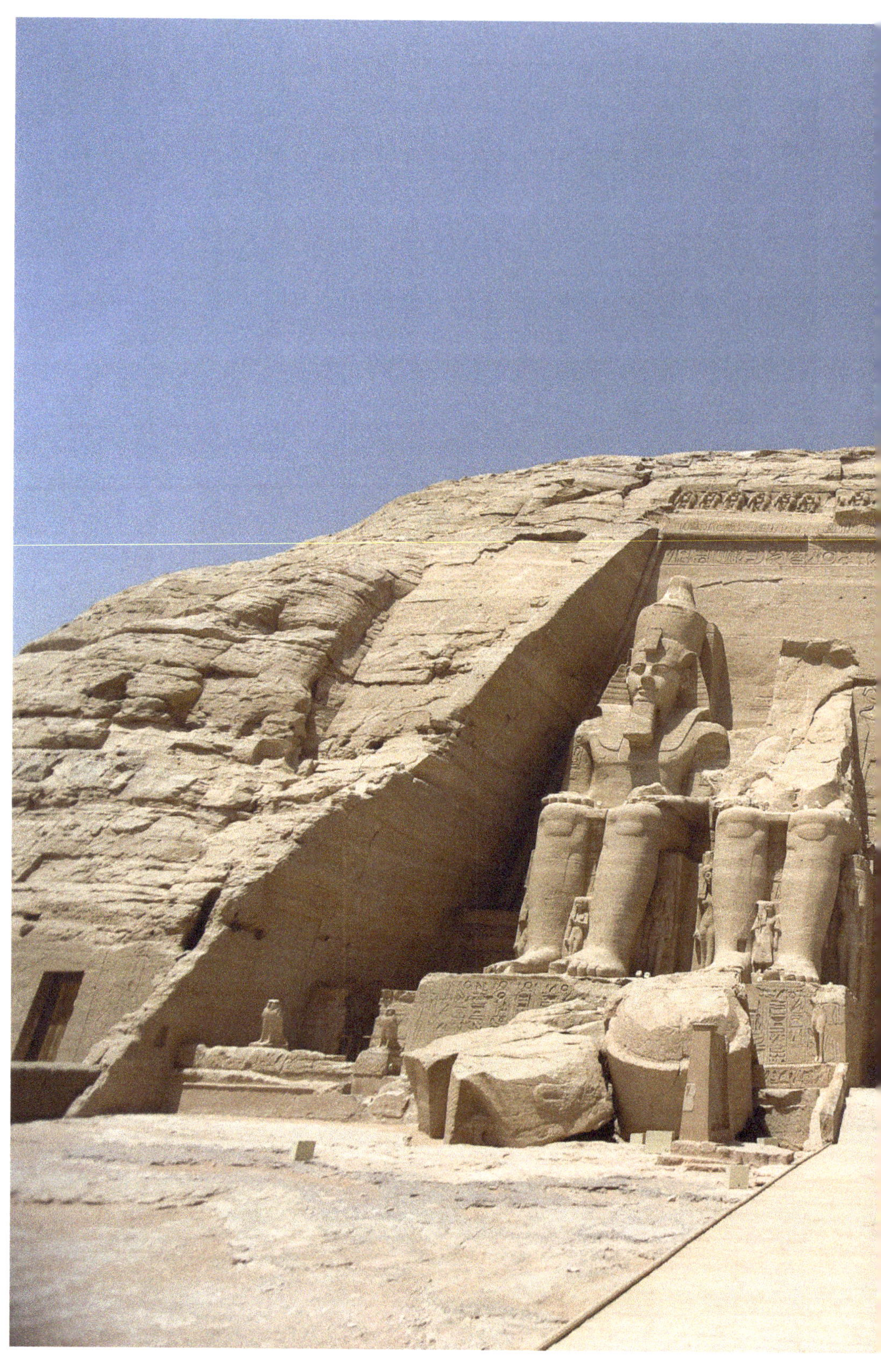

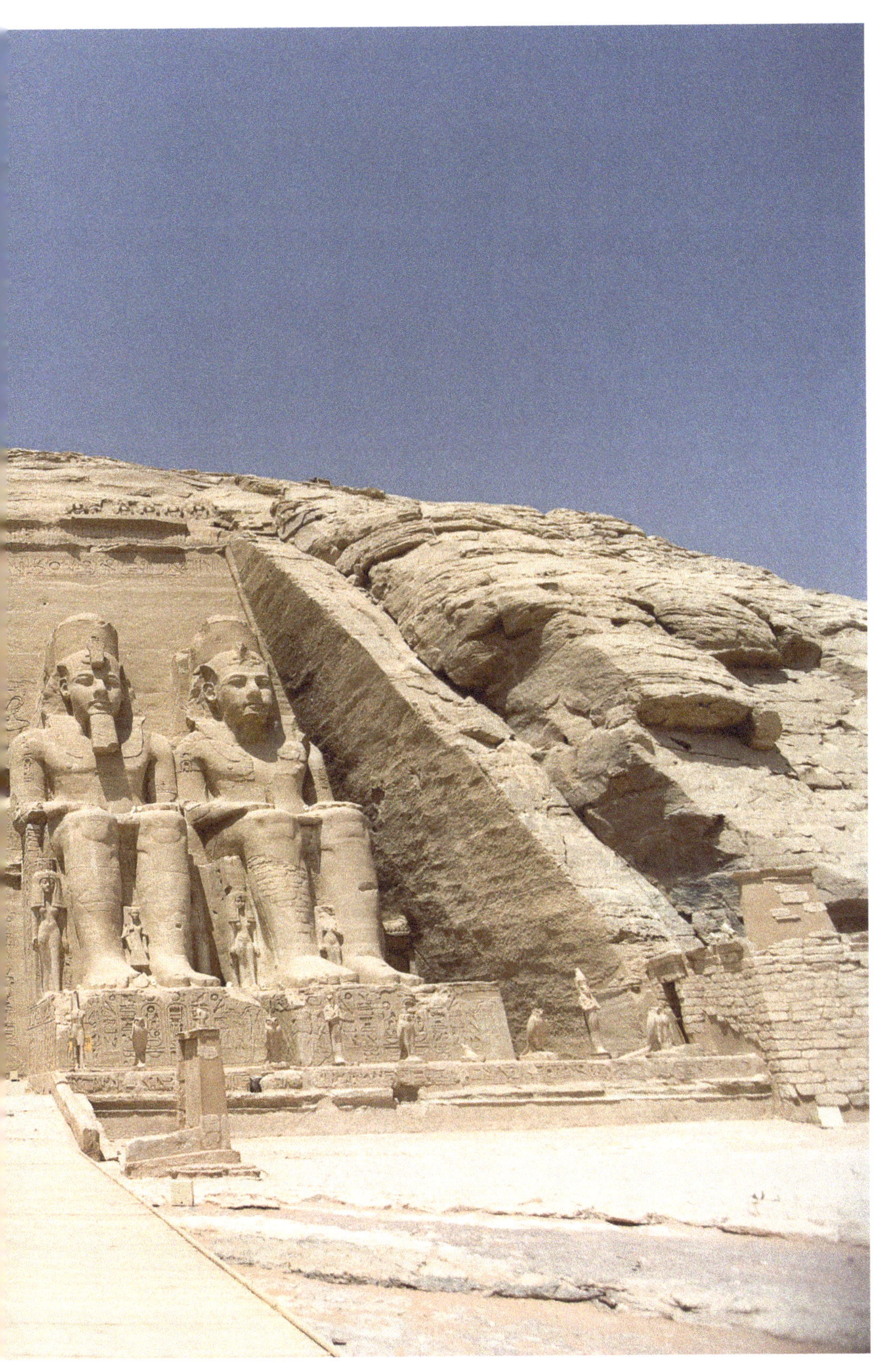

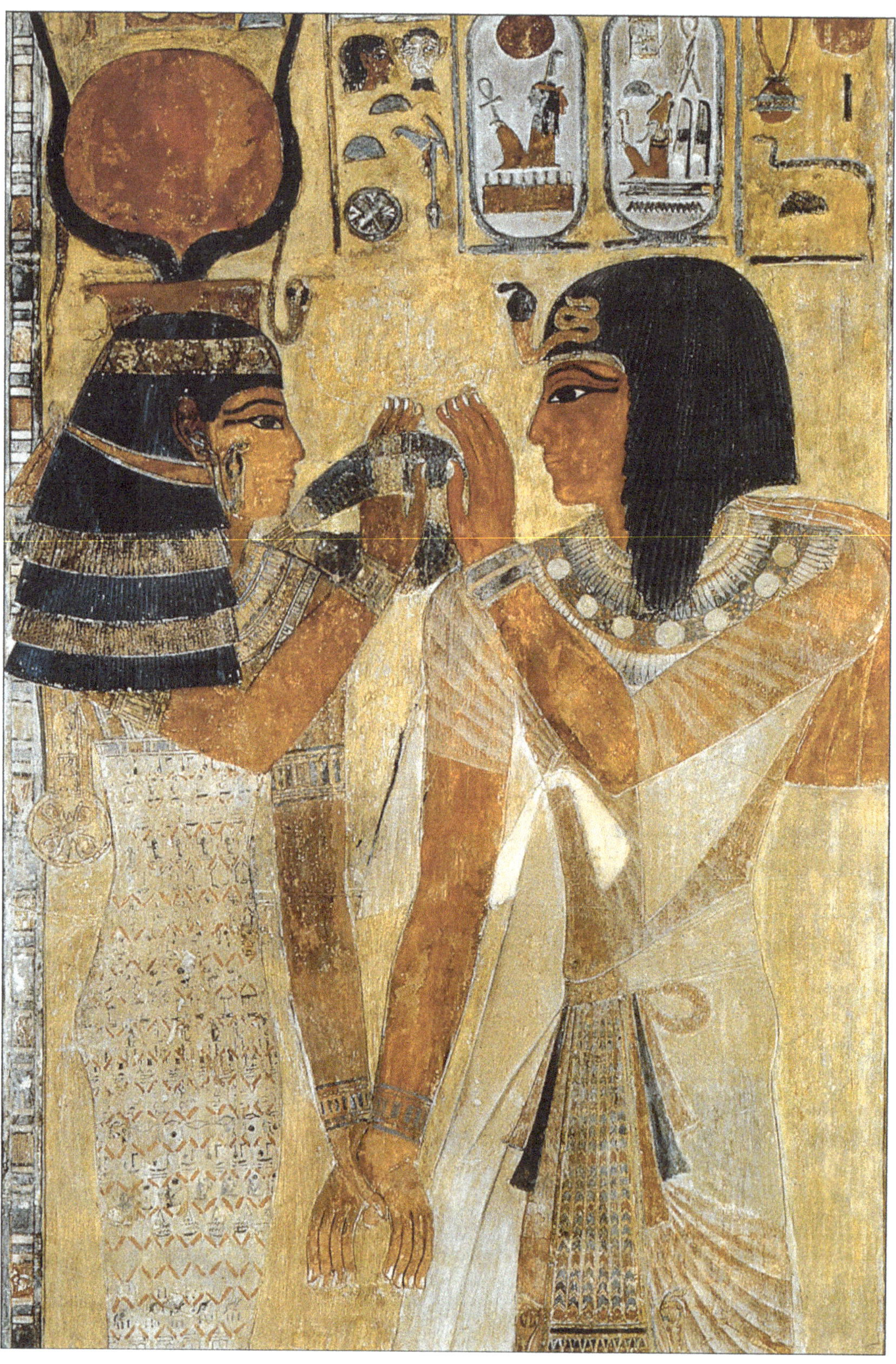

RAMESSES II, PHARAOH OF THE NINETEENTH DYNASTY.

Ra-Messu II., or Ramesses II. (c. 1303 – 1213 BCE) was the son of Seti I. and the queen Tuya, who seems to have been connected with the royal house of the Amenhotep kings. He was the third pharaoh of the Nineteenth Dynasty. The year of his age when he ascended the throne is unknown, but he is believed to have taken the throne in his late teens. He adopted as his Horus name " Mighty Bull, beloved of Maat," and a very large number of epithets which we find applied to him in the inscriptions were regarded as Horus names and treated accordingly, being placed in rectangular enclosures within which the Horus names were usually written.

Although it is improbable that Ramesses II. was crowned king of Egypt when he was still a child living in the women's quarters in the palace, we are right in thinking that he was trained with the soldiers and accustomed to military command when he was ten or twelve years of age. Besides his military appointments he held

A delicately carved and painted raised relief, originally from Seti I's tomb in the Valley of the Kings, shows Hathor embracing Seti.

the offices of counselor and overseer of certain lands, and Seti I. spared no pains to qualify him to become a wise and able prince. In the reign of Seti I. Ramesses took part in certain raids which were made upon the Libyans and other tribes living on the west and northwest frontiers of Egypt, and he was present at several fights with the Nubians in various parts of their country. He continued the wars in Nubia during the first two or three years of his reign, and they were waged with such fierceness that it seems as if some of the tribes of that country must have tried to shake off the yoke of Egypt, and to cease from the payment of tribute to the new king.

The principal memorial of his wars in Nubia, Libya, and Syria is the little rock-hewn temple at Beit al-Walli near Kalabsha, where, on the two sides of the vestibule, are scenes depicting the principal events of these wars, the capture of prisoners, and the receipt of tribute. In the Libyan war the king was accompanied by his son Amun-her-khepeshef, who is represented as bringing prisoners before his father; Ramesses was also accompanied by his favorite dog, which attacked the foe at the same time as his master. The Syrians, as usual, took refuge in their fortresses, but they availed them naught, for their entrances were forced by the Egyptian soldiers and, if we may trust the picture on the wall, the Syrians were put to the sword by the king whilst they were in the very act of tendering submission and pleading for mercy. The scenes which illustrate the Nubian campaigns are more interesting, for we see the king seated in state and receiving the gifts brought to him by the natives. These gifts consisted of gold rings, leopard or panther skins, prisoners, apes, panthers, giraffes, oxen, gazelles, ostriches, ebony, bows, feathers, fans, chairs of state, tusks of elephants, a lion, an antelope, etc., and it is clear that they must, for the most part, have been brought from the country to the south of the Fourth Cataract. On his Nubian campaign Ramesses was accompanied by his sons who are seen in their chariots charging the Nubians, and performing mighty deeds of valor. From the accounts given of the battles in Nubia it does not appear that Ramesses did anything more than make certain tribes pay tribute; he does not seem to have made his way as far to the south as some of his predecessors had done, and he certainly added no new territory to the Egyptian possessions in Nubia.

In the fourth year of his reign Ramesses was engaged in a military expedition in Syria, a fact proved by the memorial stele which he set up on the rocks overhanging the left or south bank of the Nahr al-Kalb, or "Dog River," near its mouth. Here the king is seen thrusting into the presence of the god Menthu a Syrian prisoner, who has his hands tied behind him, and whom he holds by a feather placed on the top of his head. At the Dog River there are three stelae of Ramesses II., and one of Esarhaddon, king of Assyria, who set his up on his return from the conquest of Egypt, to commemorate the capture of Memphis by him in the year B.C.E. 670. The inscriptions on all three stelae of Ramesses are obliterated and the dates of two of the three.

The Kheta wars were the chief military events of the reign of Ramesses II., and the result of them, as far as Egypt was concerned, was a reduction of her dominions. On the other hand, the arts and sciences flourished, and the noble buildings of every kind which sprang up as if by magic in all the great centers of religious thought prove that the skill of the architect, and the artist, and the workman was as great as it had ever been; their style was not so good as that of the 4th and 12th Dynasties, but this was due both to change of ideas and taste among the Egyptians, and to the influence, which was exerted on the arts and crafts by foreign intercourse and trafficking. When Ramesses II. died he left his country in a comparatively flourishing condition, but his empire was crumbling away, and the events, which took place under Merneptah prove that the nations around were only waiting for his death to invade Egyptian territory.

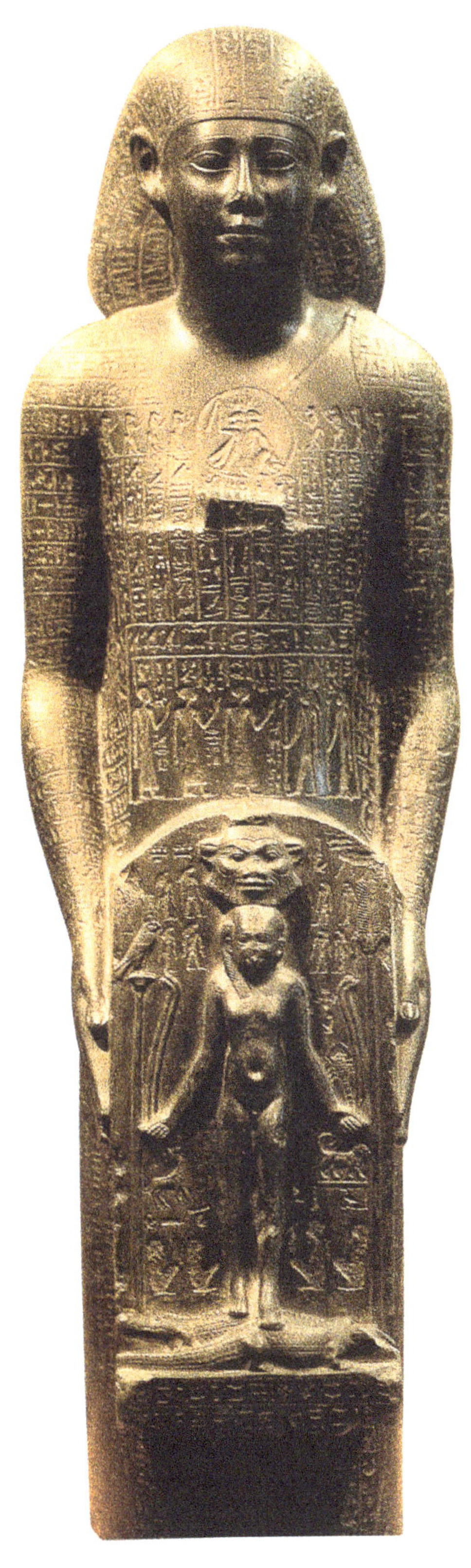

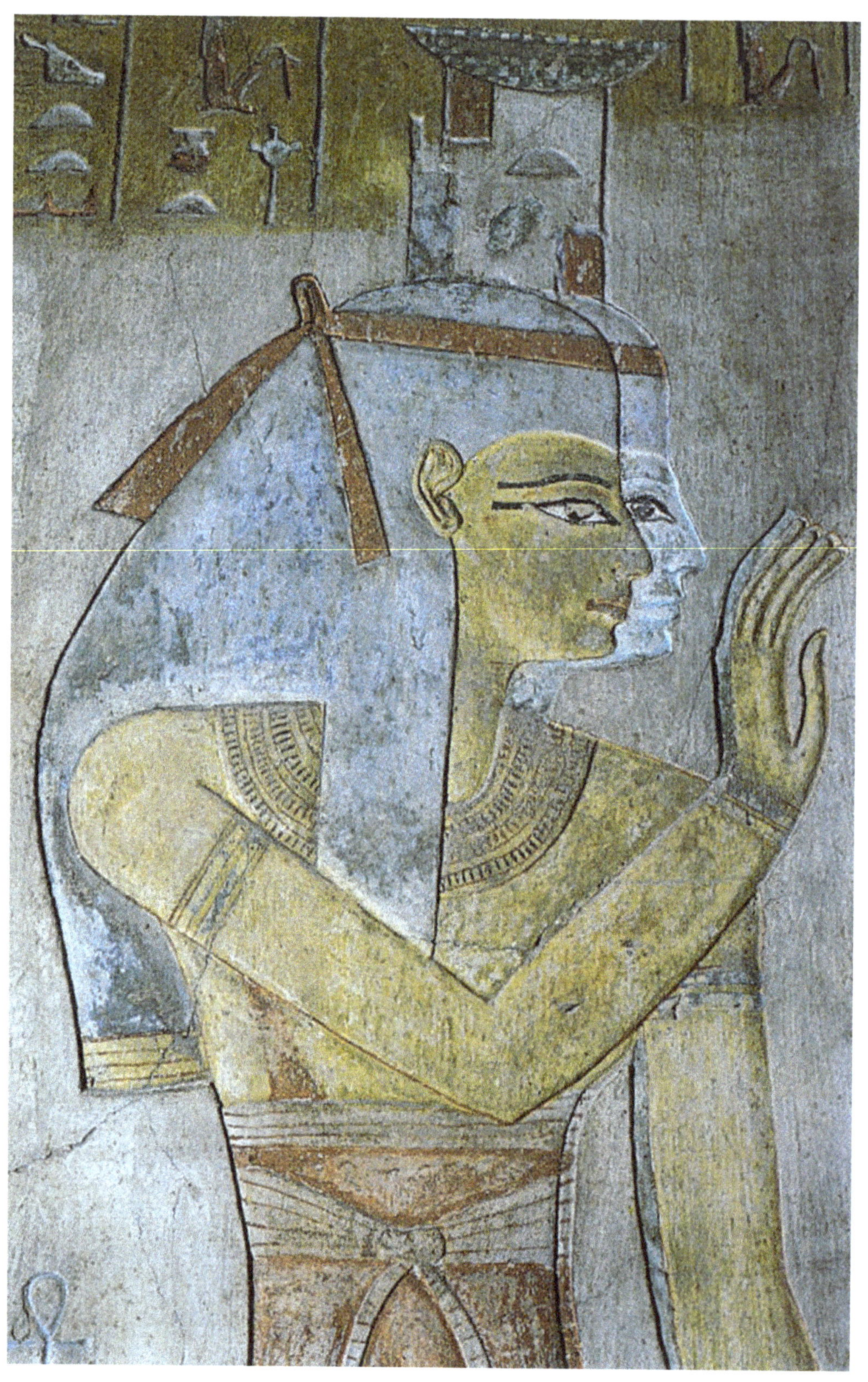

THE TWENTIETH DYNASTY

The famous temple at Abu-Simbel, which is entirely excavated out of the living rock, with its colossal statues fifty feet high, is a worthy architectural fellow to the temple of Karnak. In the 20th dynasty the imposing mass of Medinet Habu, raised to the glory of Ramesses III, bears eloquent testimony that the greatest traditions were still flourishing at that time.

The hosts of New Empire tombs at Thebes and Tell-el- Amarna furnish us with types of quite a long series of architectural styles. In some cases, the sand has so acted as a preservative that we can find the structures almost in the state in which the Egyptians left them: such, for example, is the case of the central bay of the tomb of Ay at Tell-el- Amarna. The temples, as well as the tombs, have handed down to us countless statues, both of royal and of private persons, of all sizes, from huge colossi down to delicate little statuettes, and in every kind of material, displaying a surprising variety of different attitudes and forms.

Thèbes Ouest. Vallée Des Rois. Tombe De Taousert (No 14).
Les Déesses-Sœurs Isis Et Nephthys.

It will suffice for the moment to instance one of the masterpieces of sculpture of the 18th dynasty: the Karnak statue of Tuthmosis III, or the statue of Ramesses II, presenting a table of offerings, which is at once one of the most lifelike and free productions of Egyptian art.

The court of Ramesses II at Luxor, with its great statues set up under the porticoes, proves that in spite of technical difficulties the kings did not shrink from the employment of colossi on a large scale. As may well be imagined, the walls of the temples and tombs of the New Empire have provided an incredible number of bas-reliefs, paintings and drawings. We may cite a single sketch in the tomb of Ramose at Thebes, where the artist has depicted in a group the characteristic features of the races bordering upon Egypt with a precision, which the most critical eye would find it difficult to find fault with.

The wealth of Egypt at this time did not fail to give a great stimulus to the Industrial arts: thus, the tombs have preserved for us a number of pieces of the highest order, especially furniture. Fancy articles are known, as regards the New Empire, in richer abundance than at any other period. Can one imagine any object more truly artistic in its composition than the unguent holder In the Liverpool Museum, which is made in the form of a statuette of a slave, bearing upon his shoulder a large vase?

After this spell of great abundance In the New Empire, we find ourselves almost entirely unprovided with documents for the next few centuries. The 21st to the 24th dynasties have left little by way of architecture; but as to sculpture the discovery of a hoard at Karnak has supplied us with an extensive series of statues of the chief members of the priestly families. These works are interesting certainly, but they display no particular characteristics.

Of the Saite Empire (26th and following dynasties) scarcely anything has survived. Certain statues and reliefs, however, are sufficient to testify to a renaissance, and that once more the Egyptians are drawing their inspiration from the most ancient models. In architecture, one building, the Kiosk of Nectanebo (the temple of Isis) in the island of Philae, is the introduction to the long series of Greco-Roman monuments. The Ptolemies, and then the emperors, did in fact, raise important buildings in different parts of Egypt, which are quite enough to show how much vitality the ancient art of the Pharaohs still possessed. In their day, and in this connection, it is sufficient to cite the well-known names of Philae, Edfu and Denderah. There we shall find buildings almost intact in some parts, and the study of these makes it possible for us to restore, at least

in spirit, the great ruins of the preceding ages. When one paces the pathway around the temple of Edfu, or wanders among the columns of the hypostyle hall at Denderah, one might easily be tempted to imagine that time had stopped for hundreds of years, and that one would see, without much surprise, the Egyptian priests, with their white robes and close-shaven heads, sally forth from one or other of the chambers.

The bas-reliefs, of almost infinite extent, show us the Greek dynasts or the Roman emperors doing their best to look like the native Pharaohs, their far-off predecessors. The execution has unfortunately fallen short of its intentions, and sculpture in relief, as opposed to architecture, betrays the imminent decline into which Egyptian art was soon to lapse.

Ancient egypt images on wall in Luxor Temple of Hatshepsut.

THE VALLEY OF THE KINGS, LUXOR, EGYPT - Wall painting and decoration of the tomb: ancient Egyptian gods and hieroglyphs in wall painting.

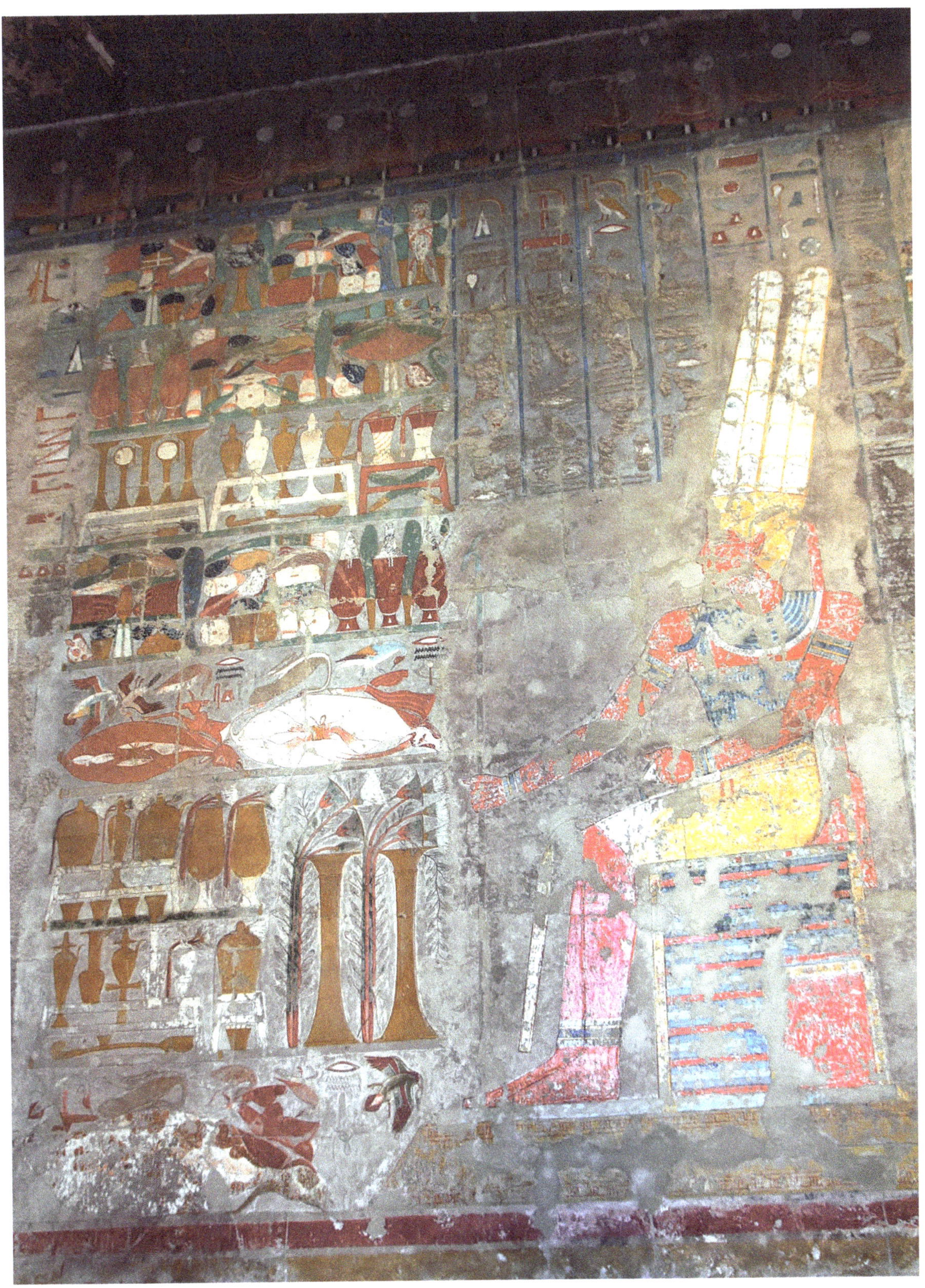

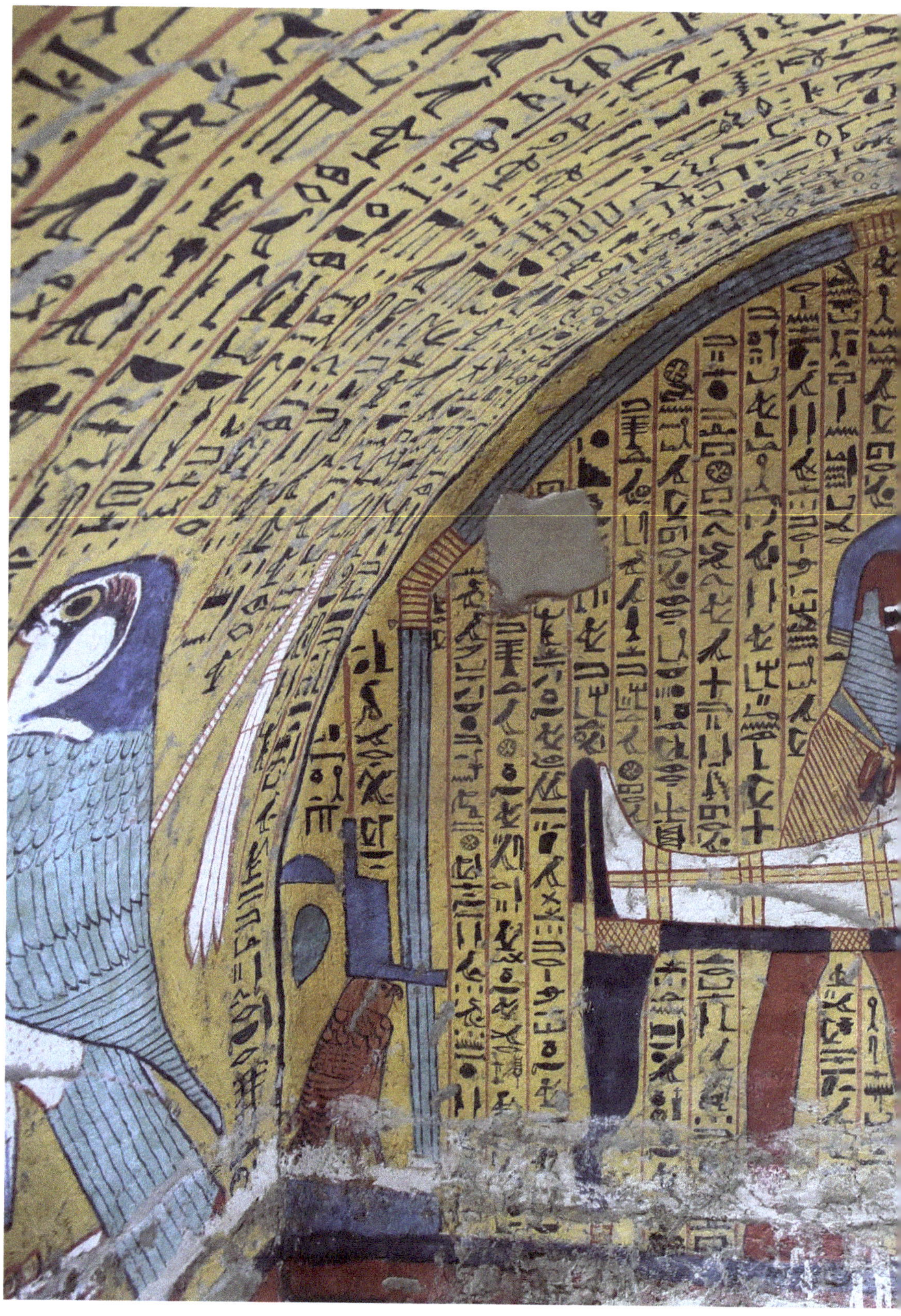

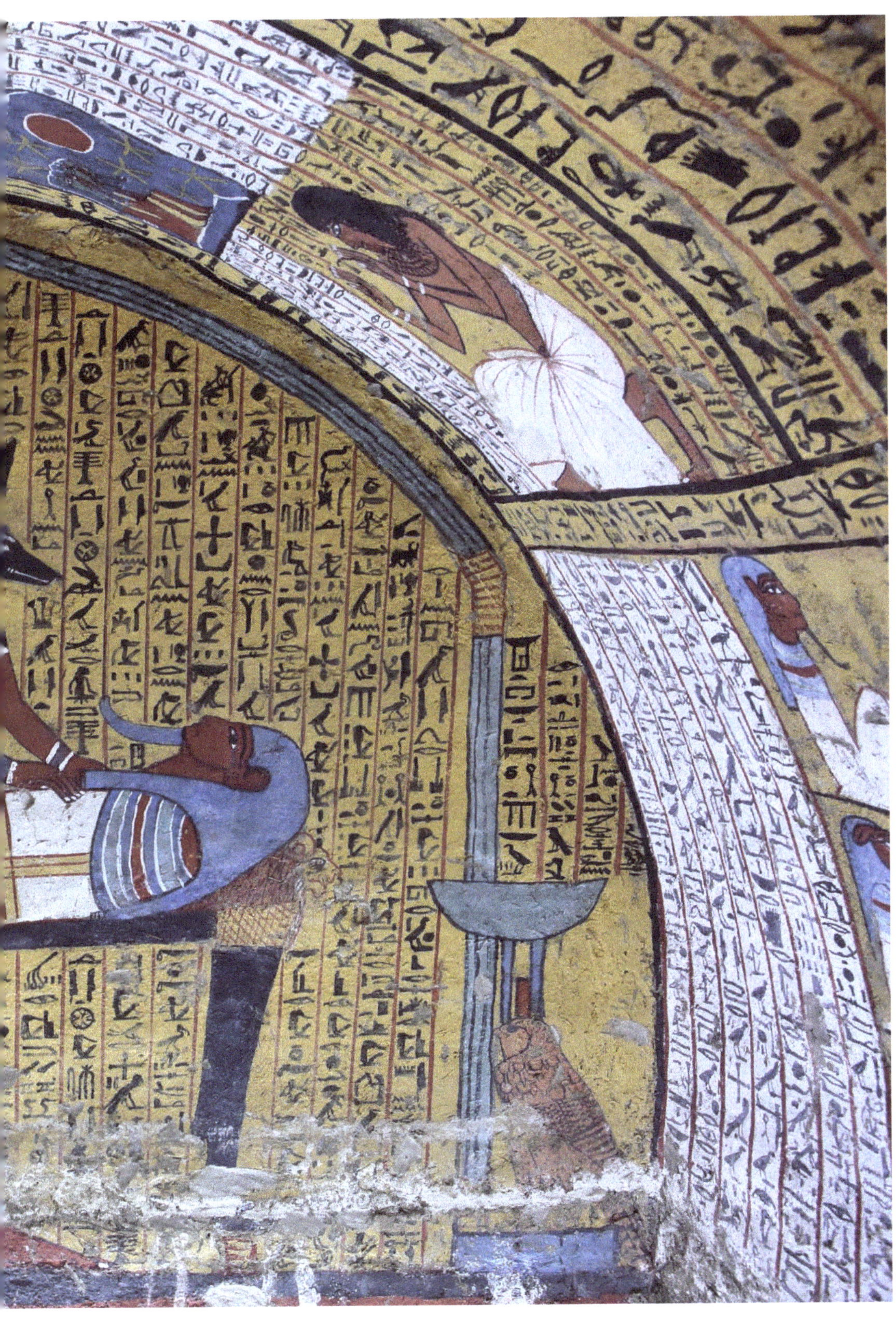

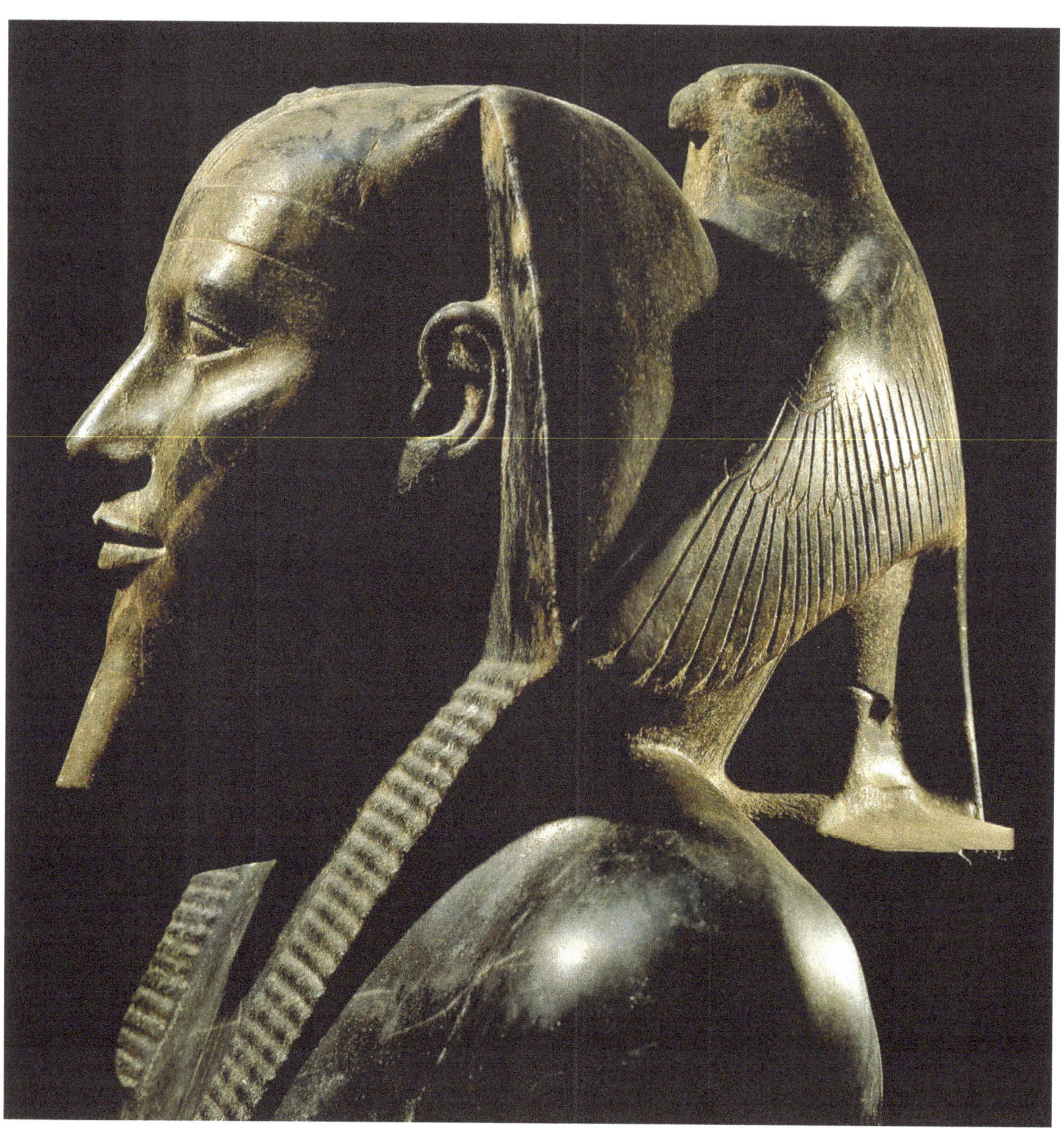

THE EGYPT THAT DOES NOT DIE

Egypt is the first of those undulations which civilized societies make on the surface of history — undulations that seem to be born of nothingness and to return to nothingness after having reached a summit.

She is the most distant of the defined forms which remain upon the horizon of the past. She is the true mother of men. But although her achievement resounded throughout the whole duration and extent of the ancient world, one might say that she has closed herself within the granite circle of a solitary destiny. It is like a motionless multitude, swelled with a silent clamor.

Egypt sinks without a cry into the sand, which has taken back, successively, her feet, her knees, her thighs and her flanks, with only her breast and brow projecting. The sphinx has still, in his crushed visage, his inexorable eyes, outlined by rigid lids, which look inward as well as outward into the distance, from elusive abstractions to the

In the valley temple, this diorite statue of King Khafre protected by the hawk god Horus is a masterpiece of Egytian art.

circular line where the curve of the globe sinks downward. To what depth do his foundations go, and how far around him and below him does history descend? He seems to have appeared with our first thoughts, to have followed our long effort with his mute meditation, to be destined to survive our last hope.

We shall prevent the sand from covering him entirely because he is a part of our earth, because he belongs to the appearances amid which we have lived, as far back as our memories go. Together with the artificial mountains with which we have sealed the desert near him, he is the only one of our works that seems as permanent as the circle of days, the alternation of the seasons, and the stupendous daily drama of the sky.

The immobility of this soil, of this people whose monotonous life makes up three quarters of the adventure of humanity, seems to have demanded lines of stone to bind it, and these lines define the soil and the people even before we know their history. Everything around the pyramids endures. The desire felt there to seek and give form to eternity, imposes itself on the mind — the more despotically since nature retards death itself in its necessary acts of transformation and recasting. The granite is unbroken.

Beneath the soil are petrified forests. In that dry air, wood that has been abandoned retains its living fibers for centuries, cadavers dry up without rotting. The inundation of the Nile, the master of the country, symbolizes, each year, perpetual resurrection. Its rise and fall are as regular as the apparent march of Osiris, the eternal sun, who arises each morning from the waters and disappears each evening in the sands. From the 10th of June to the 7th of October he pours on the calcined countryside the same fat, black mud, the mud which is the father of life.

The Egyptian people never ceased to contemplate death. It offered the spectacle without precedent, and without another example to follow it, of a race intent for eighty centuries on arresting the movement of the universe. It believed that organized forms alone died, amid an immovable nature. It accepted the world of the senses only so long as it seemed to Middle Empire. Scribes endure. It pursued the persistence of life in its changes of aspect. It imagined alternate existences for itself. And the desire all men have to survive mortal death caused the Egyptians to endow the soul with that individual eternity of which the duration of cosmic phenomena gave them the vain appearance.

In their estimation man entered upon his true life yet death. But, no less than in all the conceptions

of immortality which succeeded theirs, did the desire of the Egyptians for immortality escape the irresistible need to assure a material envelope to the ever-living spirit.

It was, therefore, necessary to construct a secret lodging, where the embalmed body should be sheltered from the elements, from beasts of prey, and especially from men. It must have with it its familiar objects — food and water; it was necessary above all that its image, the unchangeable envelope of the double which should not leave it again, should accompany it into the final shadow. And since nothing dies, it was necessary to shelter forever the symbolic divinities expressing the immutable laws and the resurrection of appearances — Osiris, fire, and the heavenly bodies, the Nile and the sacred animals which regulate the rhythm of their migration by the rhythm of its tides and its silences.

Egyptian art is religious and funerary. It began with the strangest collective madness in history. But since its poem to death lives, it touches the highest wisdom. The 'artist saved the philosopher. Temples, mountains raised by the hands of men, the Nile's own cliffs cut into sphinxes, into silent figures, dug out into labyrinthine hypogea, make a living alley of tombs to the river.

Egyptian Great Sphinx full body portrait with head feet with all pyramids of Menkaure Khafre Khufu in Giza Egypt.

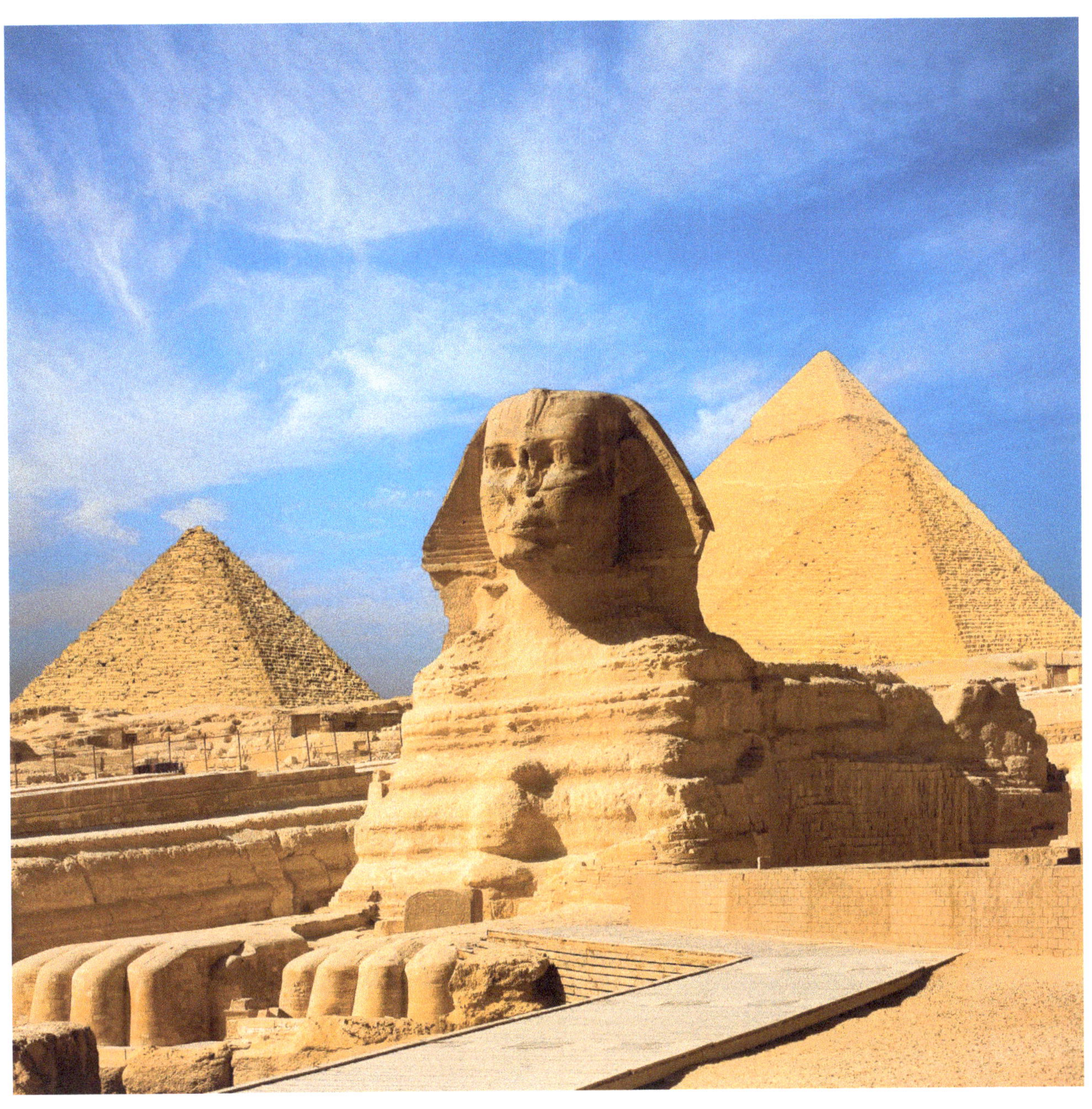

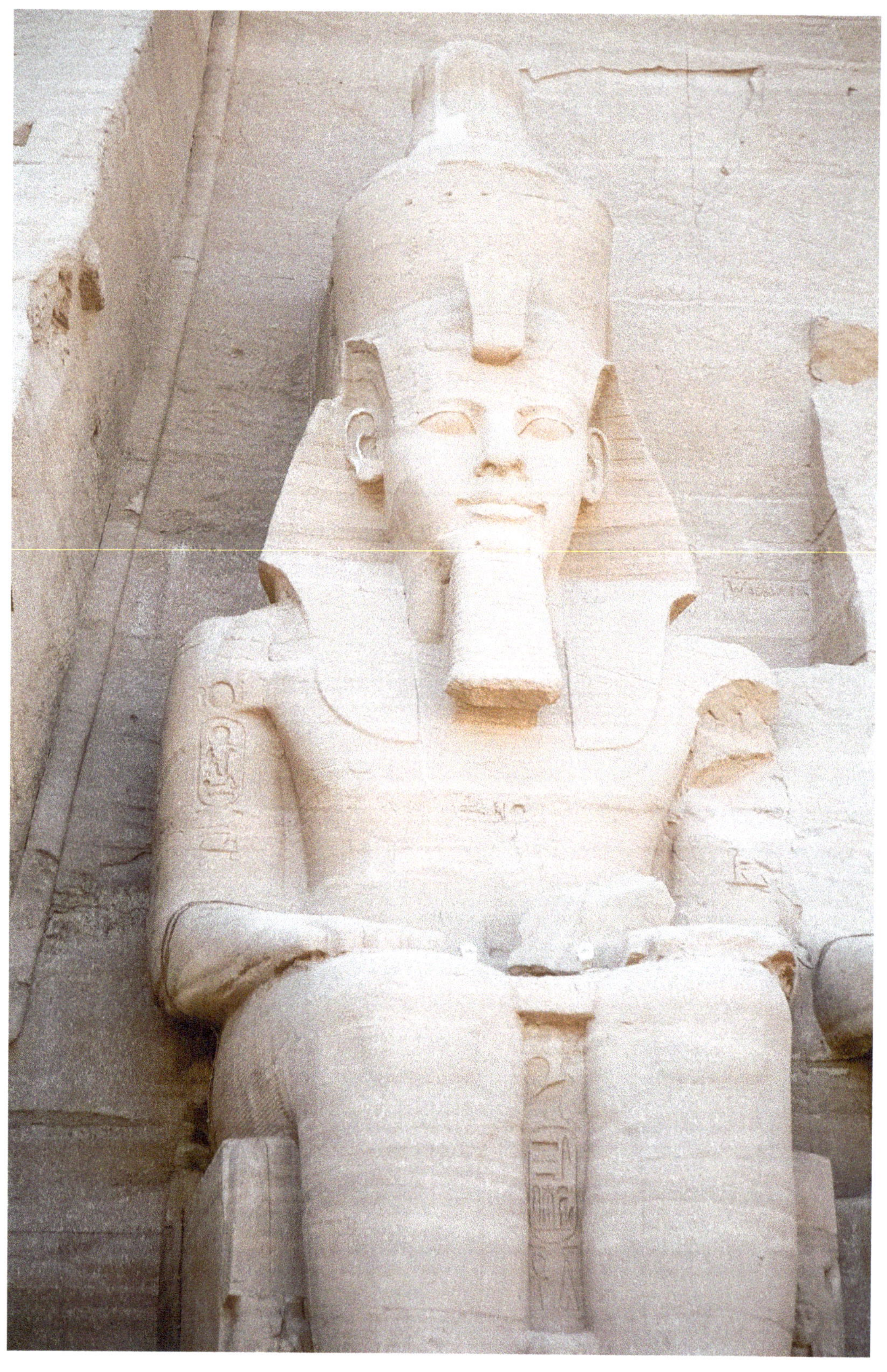

All Egypt is there, even present-day Egypt which has required the most unchanging of the great modern religions; all Egypt, with its broken enigmas, its cadavers buried like treasures, perhaps a billion mummies lying in the darkness. And that Egypt which wanted to eternalize its soul with its bodily form is dead.

The Egypt that does not die is the one which gave to stoneware, to granite, and to basalt the form of its mind. Thus, the human soul perishes with its human envelope. But as soon as it is capable of cutting its imprint in an external material— stone, bronze, wood, the memory of generations, the paper which is recopied, the book, which is reprinted and which transmits from century to century the heroic word and the songs— it acquires that relative immortality which endures so long as those forms shall endure in which our world has continued long enough to permit us to define it, and, through those forms, to define ourselves.

The temple, which sums up Egypt, has the categorical force of the primitive syntheses which knew no doubt, and by that very fact expressed the only truth we know as durable — that of instinctive life in its irresistible affirmation.

Formed by the oasis, the Egyptian soul repeated the essential teachings of the oasis on the walls and in

the columns of the temple. It shaped the granite of the temple into rectangular masses which rose in a block to the hard line of the angles, with the profile of the cliffs, with the straight-lined course of the river, with the hot sap that made the palm trees tower over the fields of emerald, of gold, and of vermilion.

The priests know much. They know the movements of the heavens. They arrange the temple as an observatory, protected by lightning conductors. They possess the great principles of geometry and triangulation. But their science is secret.

All that these people know of it is revealed by certain tricks of spiritualism and of magic which mask the sometimes puerile and often profound meaning of the occult philosophy which the hieroglyphs and the symbolic figures are meant to eternalize on the face of the desert.

The Pharaoh, the human form of Osiris, is the instrument of the theocratic caste— which overwhelms him with power so as to domesticate him. Below it and him with some intermediaries, officers, chiefs of cities or of villages, governors armed with their batons, is the multitude.

For a few hours of repose in the burning night, on the ground of hardened mud, for bread and water, they have nothing but the life of the enslaved plowman or reaper, mason or stonecutter— forced labor and blows. A hundred generations are used up to build the pyramids, men are broken at tasks beyond the strength of man, women are deformed before their age because they have been too miserable and have borne too many children, children are turned aside and warped before birth under the weight of a servitude centuries old. A frightful nightmare. In the far background there is the bare hope of future metamorphoses, a troubled and flickering light for the poor man who will have no tomb.

How is it that, in this hell, the Egyptian did not seek and find the dangerous consolation of absolute spiritualism? The living desire is stronger than death. Naturalistic and polytheistic from its origin, his religion retained the love of the form upon which we base our hope. His statues gave to mystery an indestructible skeleton, and he never adored his gods save under animal or human forms. The surroundings in which he had to live did not permit him to become absorbed in unrestrained contemplation. The daily struggle for bread is the surest of positivist educations. As a matter of fact, nature is ungrateful in Egypt.

It is only by incessant effort and thanks to resources constantly renewed, in their ingenuity and courage, that the Egyptian learned to utilize to his profit the periodical excesses of the Nile.

He had to put into practice a study, centuries old, of the habits of the river, of the consistency and the qualities of the mud; he had to undertake formidable works, dikes, embankments, artificial lakes, irrigating canals, the cutting of sandstone and of granite; he had to continue these works ceaselessly and begin them again to prevent them from being buried under the deposits of the river, from being swallowed up and disappearing. The pyramids reveal the incomparable power of his engineers. And if the hardness of his life turned his mind toward death, at least during his passage over the earth he left the impress of a profound genius for geometry.

The copper inlay around the eyes of this painted statue from the 5th Dynasty represents the green malachite scribes wore to protect their eyes.

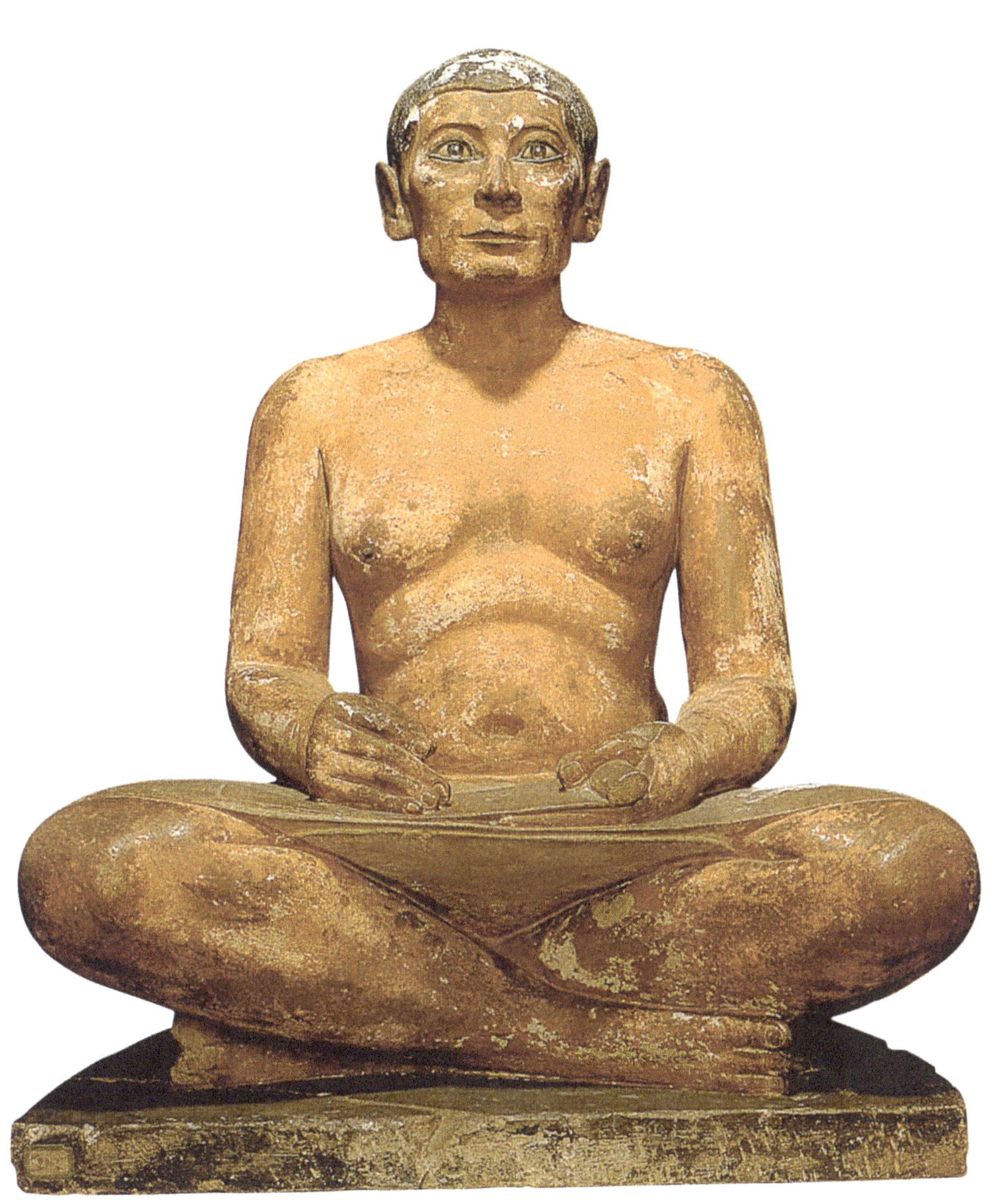

53

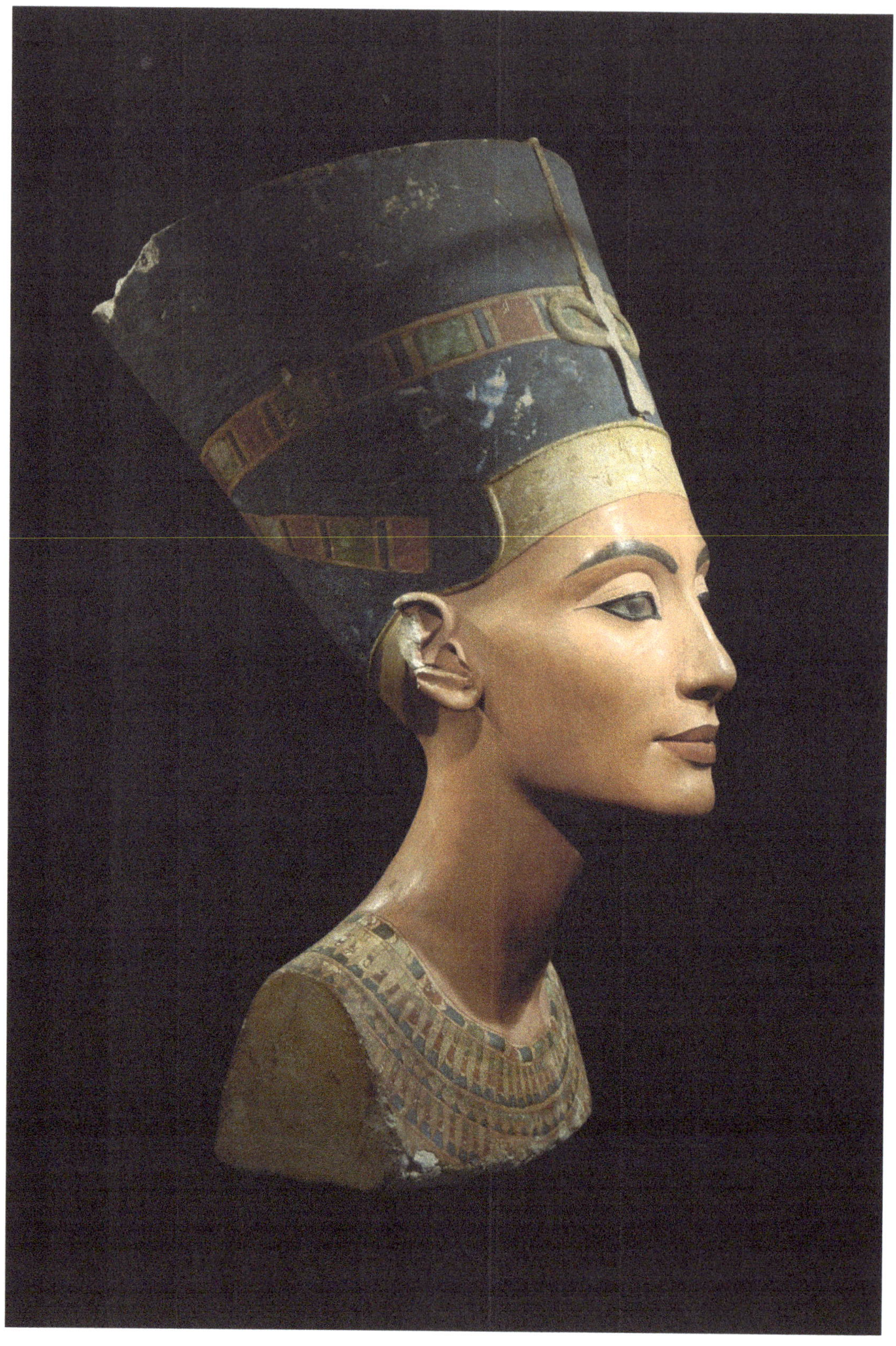

EPILOGUE

The Egyptian artist is a workman, a slave who works under the baton like the others; he is not initiated into the mystic sciences. We know a thousand names of kings, of priests, of war chiefs, and of city chiefs; we do not know one name of those who have expressed the real thought of Egypt that, which lives forever in the stone of the tombs. Art was the anonymous voice, the mute voice of the crowd, ground down and observing within itself the tremor of the mind and of hope. Sustained by an irresistible sentiment of the life it was forbidden to spread out, it allowed that sentiment to burn — with all the power of its compressed faith — into depth.

It is not true — startling and illuminating as are the metaphysical intuitions that, with their power, the priestly castes pass on through time, in Egypt as in Chaldea — it is not true that the mysterious images which symbolize these intuitions owe to them their beauty. With the artist, instinct is at the beginning of everything. It is life, in its prodigious movement wherein matter and mind merge without his thinking of disuniting them, that lights the spark in him and directs his hand. It is for us to disengage from the work of art its general signification as we disengage it from sensuous, social, and moral life, which it sums up for us in a flash. The Egyptian artist followed certain ideas, more often restrictive than active, which the priest dictated to him. When the priest demanded that a lion with a human head be cut in granite, or a man with the head of an eagle and open hands through which the flame of the spirit seemed to pass into the world, he jealously kept to himself the occult meaning of the form and the gestures, and the sculptor drew the enthusiasm which made the material quiver from the material alone and from the faith he had in the myths he animated. If the monster was beautiful, it was because the sculptor was living. The profound occultist counted for nothing in it, the naive artist for everything.

"We know really only what we have learned by ourselves, and personal discovery is our sole source of enthusiasm. The highest generalizations

Néferneferuaten Néfertiti (c. 1370-c. 1330 BC) was an Egyptian queen and the Great Royal Wife of Akhenaten, an Egyptian Pharaoh. Néfertiti and her husband were known for a religious revolution, in which they worshiped one god only, Aten, or the sun disc.

have started with the most obscure and strongest sentiment, to purify themselves step by step as they rise to intelligence. They are open to the artist who must, logically and fatally, take his course toward them. But the faculty of giving life to the language in which philosophers communicate these generalizations to us is not logically and fatally imparted to the intellectual. The generalization is never a point of departure, it is a tendency; and if the artist had begun with occultism, his work would have been condemned to the stiffness of death. Now, even when stiff as a cadaver, by the will of the priest, the Egyptian statue lives through the love of the sculptor. Only human evolution proceeds in a block, and the instinct of the artist accords with the mind of the philosopher in order to give to their abstract or concrete creations the same rhythm, which expresses a general need felt in common.

However that may be, it was the crowd and nothing but the crowd, which spread over the wood of the sarcophagi and over the compact tissue of the hypogea, the pure, living, colorful flowers of its soul. It whispered its life in the deep shadows so that that life should shine in the light of our torches when we open the hidden sepulchers. The fine tomb was dug out for the king or the rich man, it is true, and his was the luxurious existence to be traced on the walls, in funeral processions, in adventures of war or of hunting or in the work of the fields. He was to be shown surrounded by his slaves, by his farm workers, by his familiar animals; it was necessary to tell how his bread was made, how his beasts were cut up by the butcher, how his fish were caught, how his birds were captured, how his fruits were offered to him, and how his

wives made their toilet. And the crowd of artisans worked in obscurity; they thought to tell the charm, the power, the happiness, the opulence, and the life of the master; they told, above all, their misery, but also their fecund activity, utility, intelligence, inner wealth, and the furtive grace of their own life.

What marvelous painting! It is freer than the statuary, which is intended almost solely to render the image of the god or the deceased. Despite its abstract grand style, it is familiar, it is intimate; sometimes it turns to caricature; always it is malicious or tender, like this naturally human and good people, which is crushed little by little by theocratic force, and which descends into itself to consider its humble life. In the modern sense of the word there is no science of composition, no sense of perspective. Egyptian drawing is a writing that must be learned. But let one know it well, with its silhouettes whose heads and legs are always in profile while their shoulders and breasts are always in front view, and then see how all these stiff silhouettes move, with what ingenuousness they live, how their silence is peopled with animation and murmur! An extremely well-organized plan, sure, decisive, precise, but quivering. When the form appears, especially the nude form, or as it is divined through a transparent shirt, the artist suspends his whole life in it, that nothing but a light of the spirit may shine from his heart, one which shall illumine only the highest

The solid gold mask of Tuthankhamun was placed over the face
of the mummy.

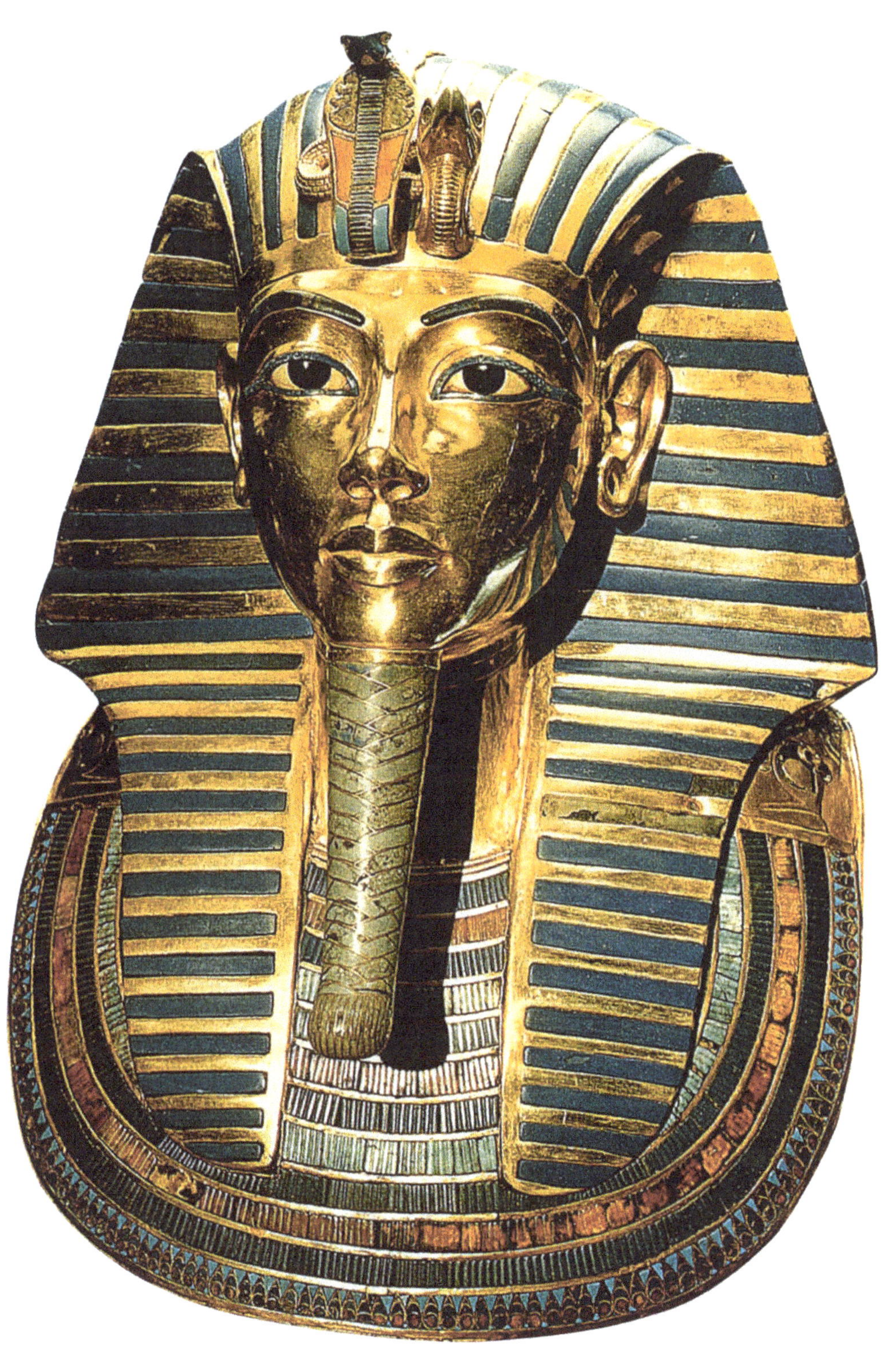

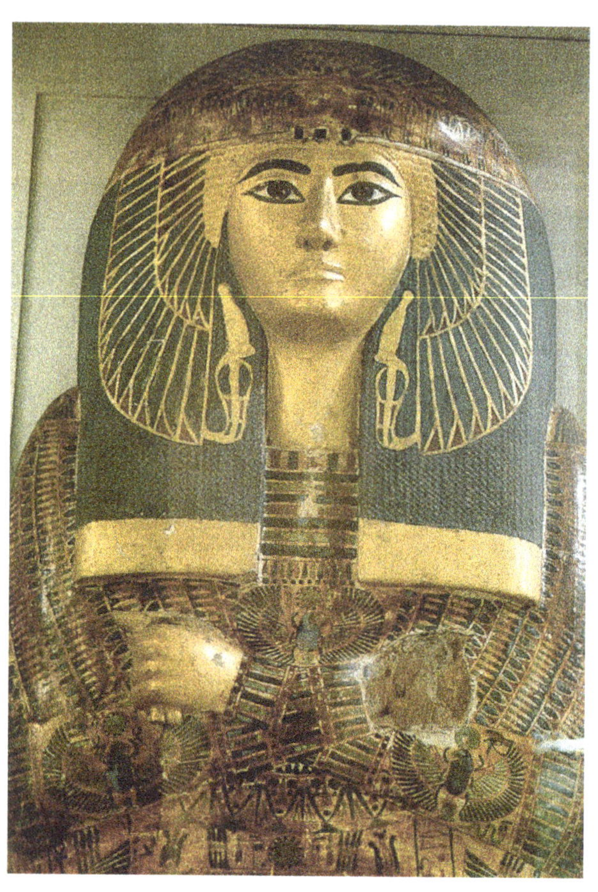

The lid of the coffin of Queen Maatkare, which as found in Deir el-Bahri. The daughter of the High Priest, she was installed as 'God's Wife of Amun', an important religious and political post.

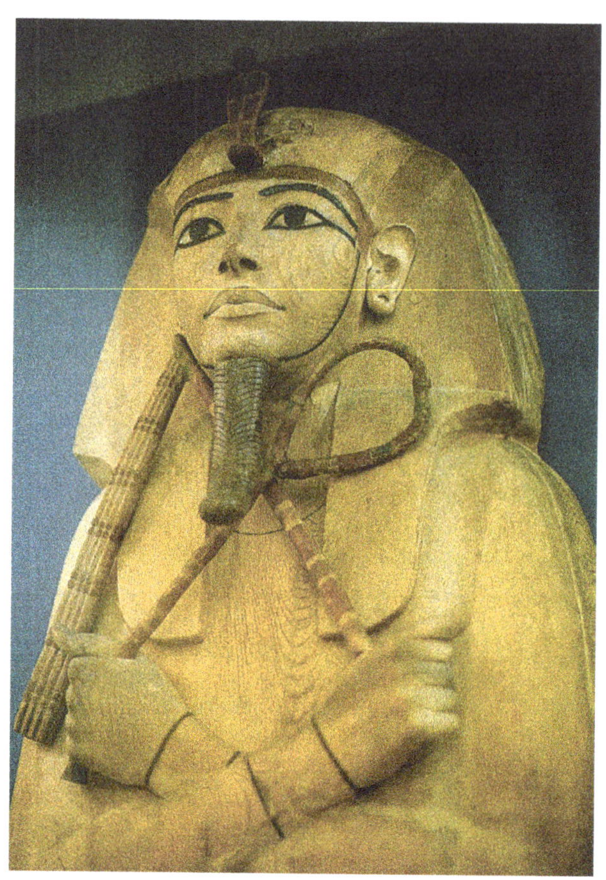

The wooden coffin, which housed the mummy of Ramesses II, found in the Deir el-Bahri cache, was possibly originally intended for Ramesses I.

Ancient egyptian sculpture of Lion of Nectanebo at the Cortile della Pigna (Pinecone courtyard) of the Vatican Museums.

summits of memory and of sensation. Truly, that continuous contour, that single undulating line, so pure, so nobly sensual, which evinces so discreet and strong a sense of character, of mass, and of movement, has the appearance of being traced in the granite by the intelligence alone, without the help of a tool. Then come streaming the deep blues, emeralds, ochers; golden yellows, and vermilions —lightly, never thickly applied. It is like perfectly clear water into which one would drop, without stirring it by a tremor, unchangeable colors: they do not muddy it, but let the plants and pebbles at the bottom be seen.

Egyptian art is perhaps the most impersonal that exists. The artist effaces himself. But he has such an innate sense of life, a sense so directly moved and so limpid that everything of life which he describes seems defined by that sense, to issue from the natural gesture, from the exact attitude, in which one no longer sees stiffness. His impersonality resembles that of the grasses which tremble at the level of the ground or of the trees bowing in the wind with a single movement and without resistance, or that of the water which wrinkles into equal circles all moving in the same direction.

On the surface of the soil we get the philosophic Egypt. Only under the Ancient Empire, five or six thousand years ago, the Memphite school of sculpture essayed an expression of everyday existence. Egypt remembered old epochs of liberty, perhaps, before the sphinx himself, epochs of which we shall someday find traces under ten thousand years of alluvial deposits, lower than the foundations of the pyramids. Art, moreover, is always realistic at its beginnings. It does not yet know how to form those synthetic images, made up of the thousands of forms encountered on the long ascending road toward civilization, which art tries to realize as soon as it gets to the threshold of the general idea. Primitive man is almost solely concerned with his own life. Certainly, he makes his attempt at resumes of sensations, but at resumes of things before his eyes, not of those which pass beyond the vision of the moment. It is in order to characterize well visible forms that he leaves nothing of them but the summits of their undulations and of their expressive projections. The "Seated Scribe," which is of that ancient epoch, is of a terrifying truthfulness, in the man's direct application to the task he accomplishes. He is not yet a type of average humanity; he is already the average type of a profession and a caste. His attention to his work, his suspended energy that arrested life which makes his face flame like a torch and that animates his fixed body are due to the planes which define him, and to the trenchant mind, free of disquietude, of the man who cut them. Of the same period are the peasants who march stick in hand, the men and women who start, side by side on the voyage of death, as they embarked on the voyage of life. The Egyptian of that time possessed the equilibrium of his functions. Each wheel of the social machine acted, at that moment, with a vigor and an automatism which marked a life that was spontaneously disciplined, but free to define itself.

The classic sculpture came into existence only under the Middle Empire when Thebes had dethroned Memphis. From that moment and until

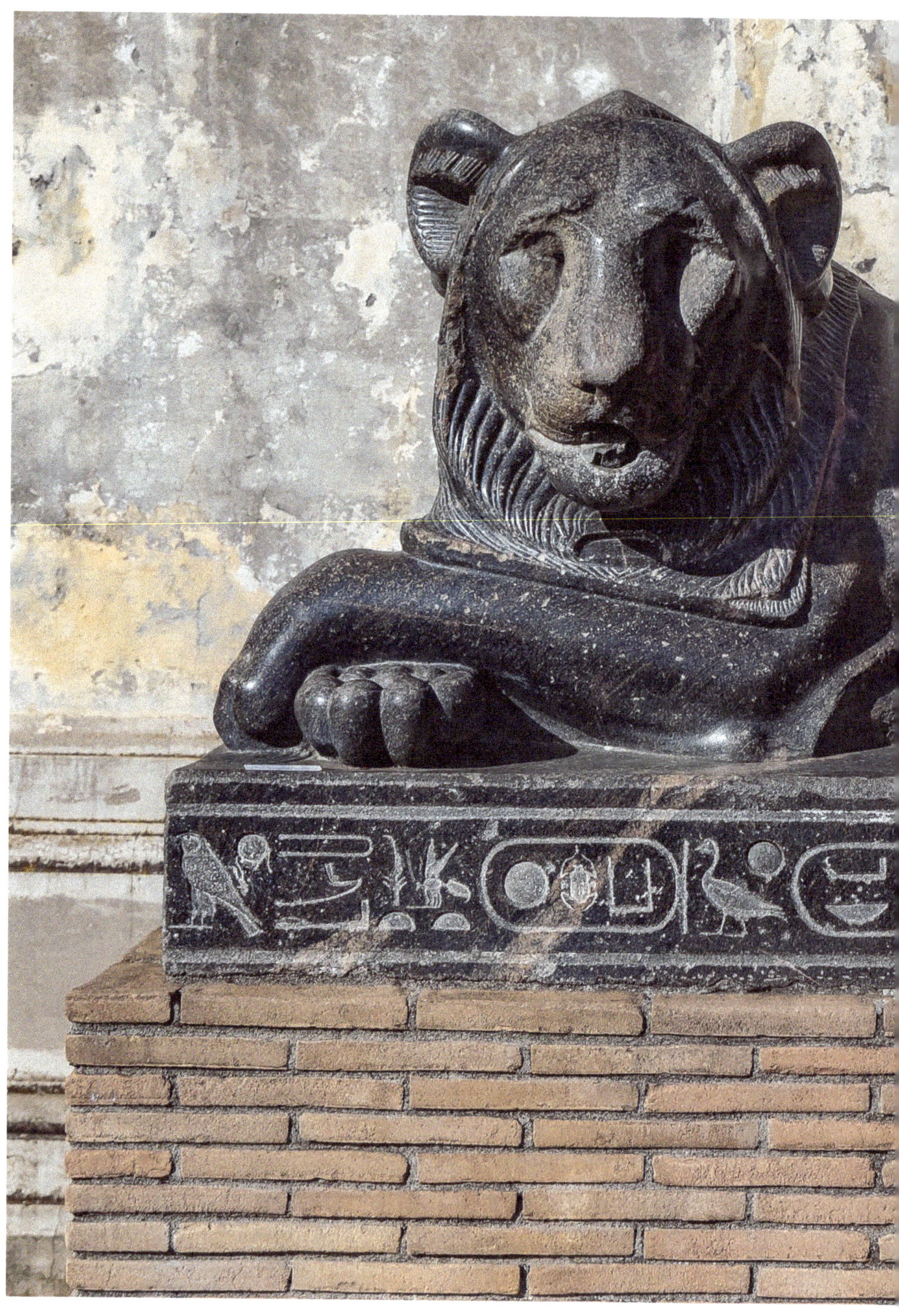

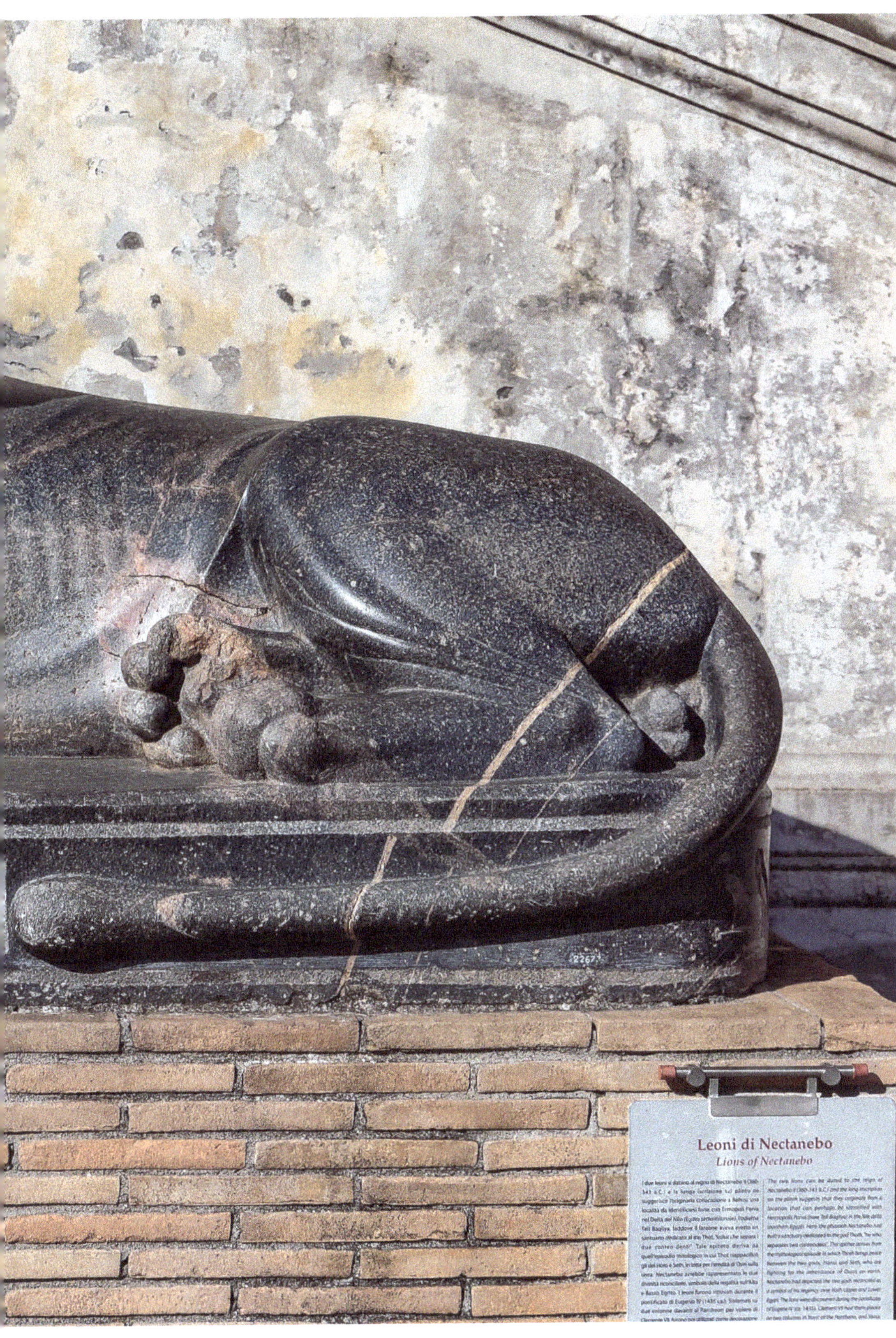
Leoni di Nectanebo
Lions of Nectanebo

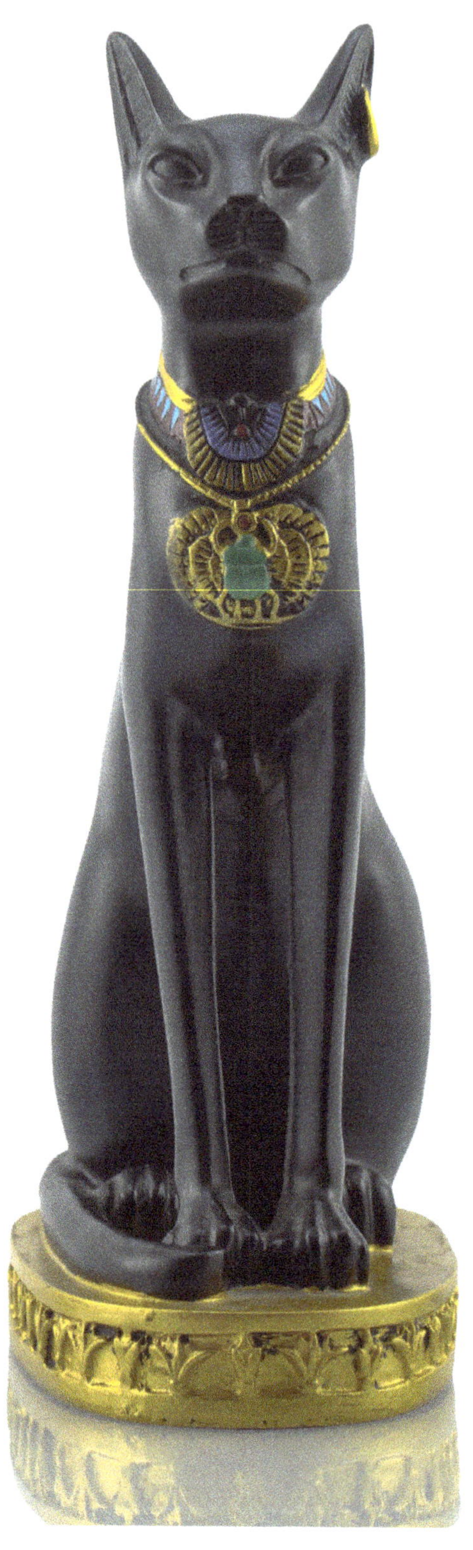

the end of the world of the Nile, it was scarcely more than funerary and religious: statues of gods and statues of doubles. The story of the harvest, of the active work of the men and animals of the plow, of boudoir and household cares, of the adventures of everyday life, was left to painting and to the workmen of art. The sculptor of the gods was indeed a workman too, but he was raised, by the importance of his task and the strength of his faith, well above his misery. One might say that he had turned his back on the oasis, that he contemplated only the regularity of the days and the years, the sleeping and the awakening of the seasons, of the river, the sad desert, the impassible face of the sky. We must not be too greatly surprised at seeing him thus different from the man who gave that account of the scribe with so much passionate attention. From afar, Egyptian art seems changeless and forever like itself. From nearby, it offers, like that of all the other peoples, the spectacle of great evolutions, of progress toward freedom of expression, of researches in imposed hieratism. Egypt is so far from us that it all seems on the same plane. One forgets that there are fifteen or twenty centuries, the age of Christianity — between the "Seated Scribe" and the great classic period, twenty-five or thirty centuries, fifty, perhaps — twice the time that

Statuette of black egyptian cat with gold isolated on white.

Egyptian Sphinx Statue isolated on white background art and illustration.

Row of ancient sphinxes at Luxor temple in Egypt.

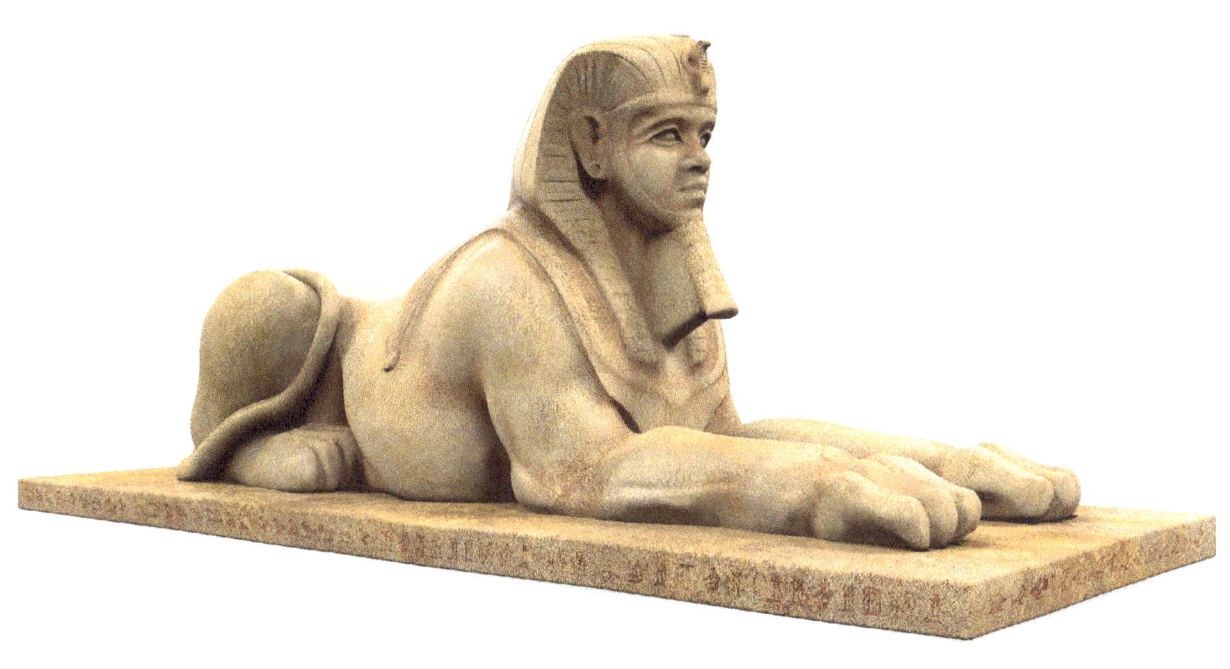

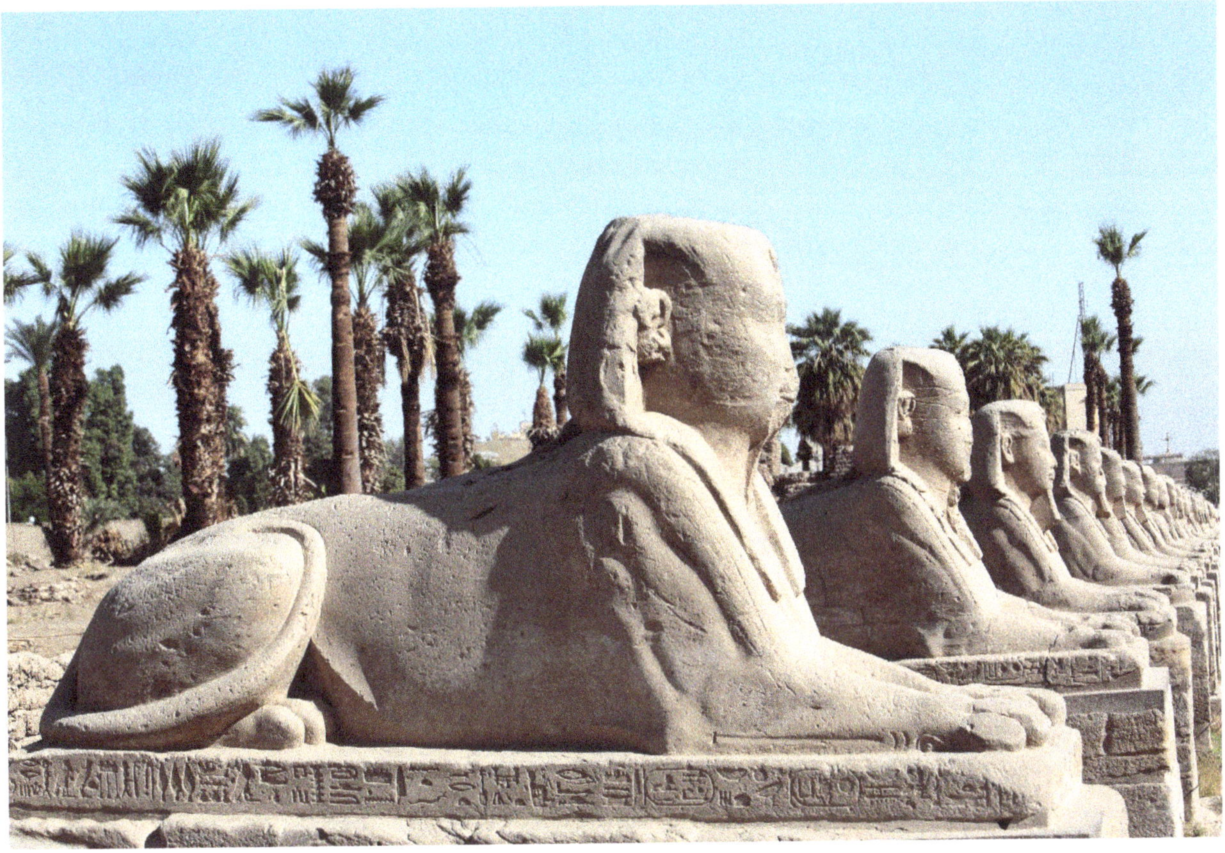

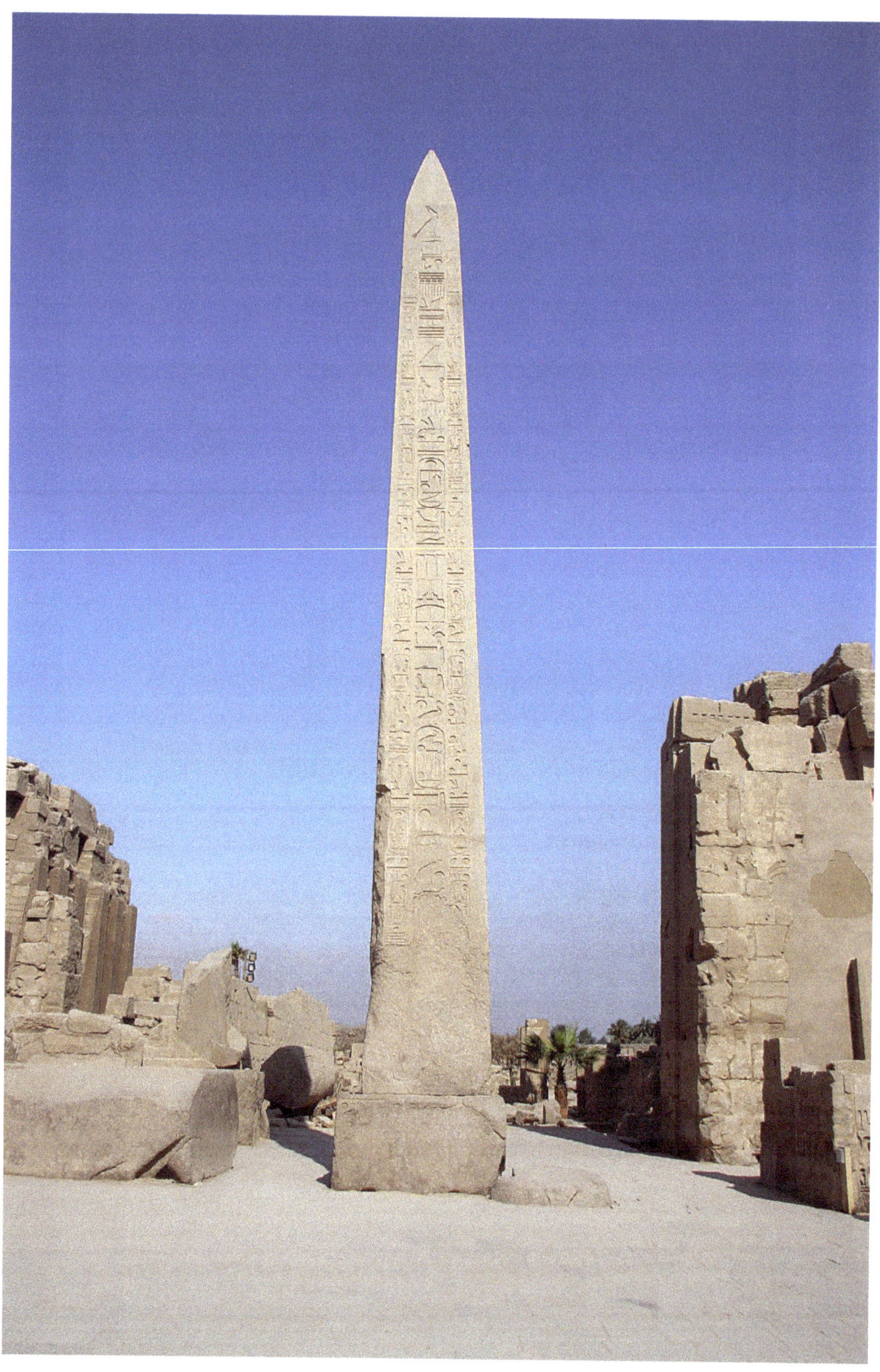

separates us from Pericles and Phidias — between the pyramids and the Saite school, the last living manifestation of the Egyptian ideal.

The statues will define the permanent aspect of Egypt, arrest life between regular dikes, cause the world to begin and end with them as the cultivated land ends and the desert begins with the limit of the river mud. Egyptian sculpture becomes a changeless architectonic frame; a century-old study of form, having penetrated the laws of its structure, has affixed this frame which will henceforth enclose the portrait of the god or the portrait of the deceased, the dwelling place of the double. Everything changes. Forms are born and effaced on the surface of the earth as easily as figures on a blackboard. There is nothing changeless save the almost mathematical relationships which animate them, binding them together with the invisible chain of abstraction. The great sculpture of Egypt materializes that abstraction and formulates in granite a geometrical ideal that seems as durable as the laws which govern the course of the heavenly bodies and the rhythm of the seasons. Sculpture is at once the most abstract and the most positive of plastic expressions — positive, because it is impossible to evade the difficulties of the task through verbal artifices and because the form will live only on condition that it be logically constructed, from whatever side one considers it; abstract, because the law of that construction is revealed to us only by a series of more and more generalized mental operations.

Karnak Temple Luxor Egypt

Before it was an art, sculpture was a science, and no sculptor can produce durable work if he has not found the generating elements of it in Nature herself. Now it was the Egyptians who taught us that, and it is perhaps not possible to understand and to love sculpture if one has not first undergone the severe education they afford us. The head of their statues remains a portrait, to which style is given by the subordination of its characteristics to a few decisive planes, but the body is molded in a canon of architectural science which will not be reached again. One foot is in front of the other or beside it; the statue, almost always crowned with the pschent, is half nude, standing with the arms glued to the sides or seated, the elbows at the thorax, the hands on the knees, the face looking straight ahead, the eyes fixed. It is forbidden to open its lips, forbidden to make a gesture, forbidden to turn its head, to arise, to leave its pedestal in order to mingle with living beings. One would say that it was tied down with bands. But yet it bears within it, in its visage, where thought wanders with the light, and in its immobilized body, the whole life spread out on the walls of the tombs, the bursting life of the shadows. A wave runs through it, a subterranean wave, whose sound is stifled. The statue's profiles have the sureness of an equation of stone and a sentiment so vast that everything of which we are in ignorance seems to reside in it silently. It will never tell its secret. The priest has enchained its arms and its legs, sewn up its mouth with mystic formulas. Egypt will not attain the philosophic equilibrium — that sense of the relative, which gives us the sense of the measure of our action and, in revealing to us our true relationships with things in their ensemble, assigns to us, in the harmony of the universe, the role of conscious center of the order which it imposes on us. She will not know the freedom toward which she was tending in the period of Memphis, and which the painters suspect as they grope about in' the darkness of the tombs.

From the beginning of the Middle Empire to the end of the New, Egypt returns to the spirit that erected the pyramids. She will cover herself with giant temples and with colossi, Ibsamboul, Luxor, Karnak, Ramesseum, piles of stone, walls, pylons, statues of disproportionate size, sphinxes, mill wheels of stone under which the king in his pride grinds the multitude which, in turn, is consoled by its pride in making gods. When the artist cuts straight from the block these absolute forms whose surfaces seem determined by geometrical volumes penetrating one another according to immutable laws of attraction, one would say that he retains, in the depth of his inexhaustible instinct, the remembrance of the common form from which all others come: animal forms, and, beyond the animal forms, those of the original sphere whence the planets issued and whose curve was sculptured by the gravitation of the heavens. The dried-out cadavers, which the soil of Egypt will finally absorb bit by bit, have not the reality of her sphinxes and her fearful gods with men's bodies and the head of hawks and panthers, where the spirit has laid its spark.

But this definitive science will eventually destroy the statue maker's art. An hour arrives when the mind, directed along a single road, can discover nothing more there. Doubtless the immobility of Egypt had never been more than an appearance. But the ideal of her mind, even if she tried to define herself in new forms, changed but little, for the teachings of her soil scarcely varied and it was always with the same surroundings that man had to reckon.

Under the Ramessides (the kings of the Twentieth Dynasty), the overstrained effort of the preceding dynasties was disunited. Continual war with outside powers, invasions, and foreign influences discouraged and unsettled the spirit of the Egyptians. After fifteen centuries of uninterrupted production, the Theban statue maker handled his material with too great facility. Occultism was, however, cultivated as much by the priestly classes and was thus the master that directed the artisan. But he had lost the power of action. He had lost that prodigious sense of mass that concentrates life in a decisive form of which all the surfaces seem to rejoin the infinite through their unlimited curves. Each year he delivered by hundreds of statues manufactured in quantity from the same commercial model. The school was formed. Geometrical idealism had fixed itself in a formula and sentiment had exhausted itself through continually encountering those unscalable walls of stone which forbade it to go farther. Egypt died of her need of eternity.

But her death was to be a slow one. She was even to have, before passing on the torch to younger hands, a fine reawakening to action. With the Saite dynasty, about the time when Greece emerged from the myth into history, she profited by the decadence of Assyria

Ancient Egyptian mummy body

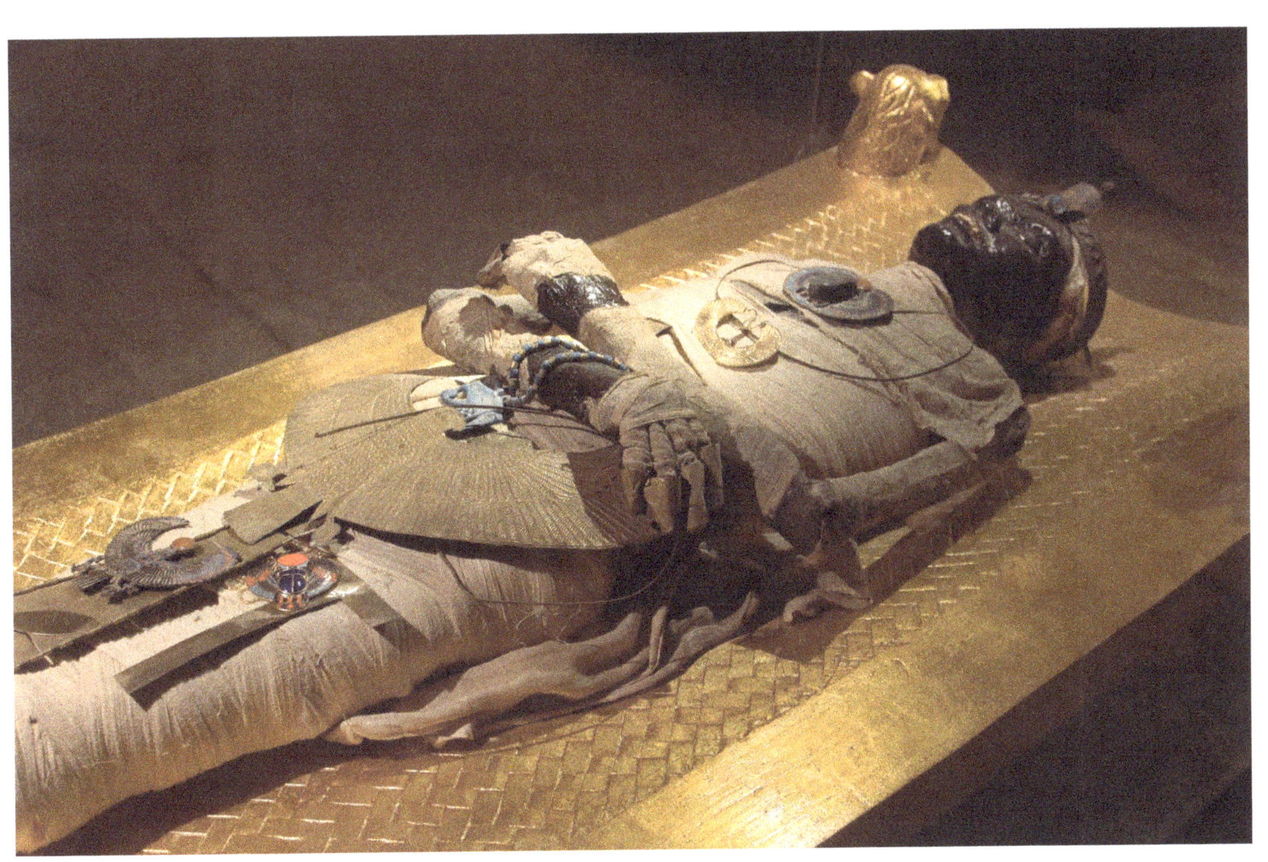

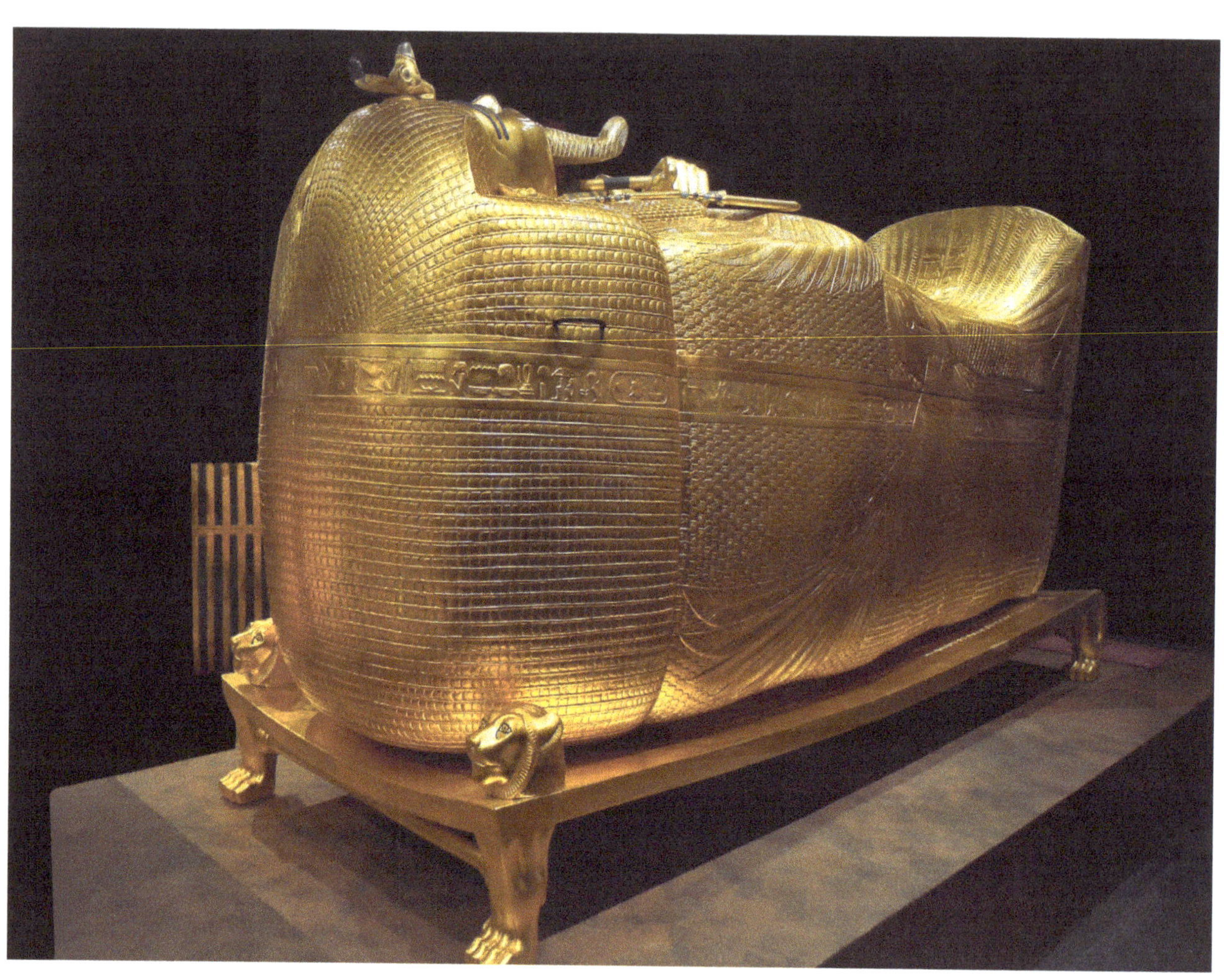

and that of the interior organization of the Medo - Persian power, to recover courage, in view of her reestablished security. Once more she looked about her and into herself, and discovered in her old soul — infused with freshness by the confused presentiment of a new ideal — a supreme flower, as warm as an autumn. She cradled nascent Greece with a farewell song, still quite virile, and very gentle.

Saite art returned to original sources. It was as direct as the ancient Memphite art. But it has almost rediscovered the science of Thebes, and if it seems softer than Theban art, it is because its tenderness is more active. Now, we no longer find only funerary statues. Saite art escapes the formula; it produces faithful portraits, precise and nervous — scribes again, statuettes of women, personages seated on the ground, their hands crossed on their knees, at the height of the chin.

In the last works, Egypt confides to us her most intimate thought about the young women and the men seated like the boundary marks of roads. Everything is a restrained caress, a veiled desire to penetrate universal life before Egypt abandoned herself unresistingly to its current. And that is all. The walls of stone that enclosed the soul of Egypt are broken by invasion, which recommences and finds her at the end of her strength. Her whole inner life runs out of the open wound. Cambyses (emperor of the Achaemenid Empire who expanded the empire into Egypt during the Late Period by defeating the Egyptian Pharaoh Psamtik III during

the battle of Pelusium in 525 B.C.E.) may overturn her colossi; Egypt cannot offer a virile protest; her revolts are only on the surface and accentuate her decline. When the Macedonian comes, she willingly includes him among her gods, and the oracle of Amnion finds it easy to promise him victory. In the brilliant Alexandrian epoch, her personal effort was practically nil. It was the Greek sages and the apostles of Judea who came to drink at her spring, now almost dried up, but still full of deep mirages, that they might try, in the unsettled world, to forge from the debris of the old religions and the old sciences a new weapon for the idea. She saw, with an indifferent eye, the dilettante from Hellas visiting and describing her monuments, and the Roman parvenu raising them again. She let the sand mount up around the temples, the mud fills the canals and bury the dikes, and the weariness of life slowly covered up her heart. She did not disclose the true depth of her soul. She had lived enclosed, she remained enclosed, shut like her coffins, her temples, her kings, a hundred cubits high, whom she seated in her oasis, above the motionless wheat, their foreheads in the solitude of the heavens. Their hands have never left their knees. They refuse to speak. One must consider them profoundly and seek in the depth of oneself the echo of their mute confidences. Then their somnolence is awakened confusedly. The science of Egypt, its religion, its despair, and its need for eternity — that endless murmur of ten thousand monotonous years — the whole of it is contained in the sigh which the colossus of Memnon exhales at sunrise.

Tutankhamen Pharaohs Ancient Egypt.

Ancient ruins of Karnak temple in Egypt at noon.

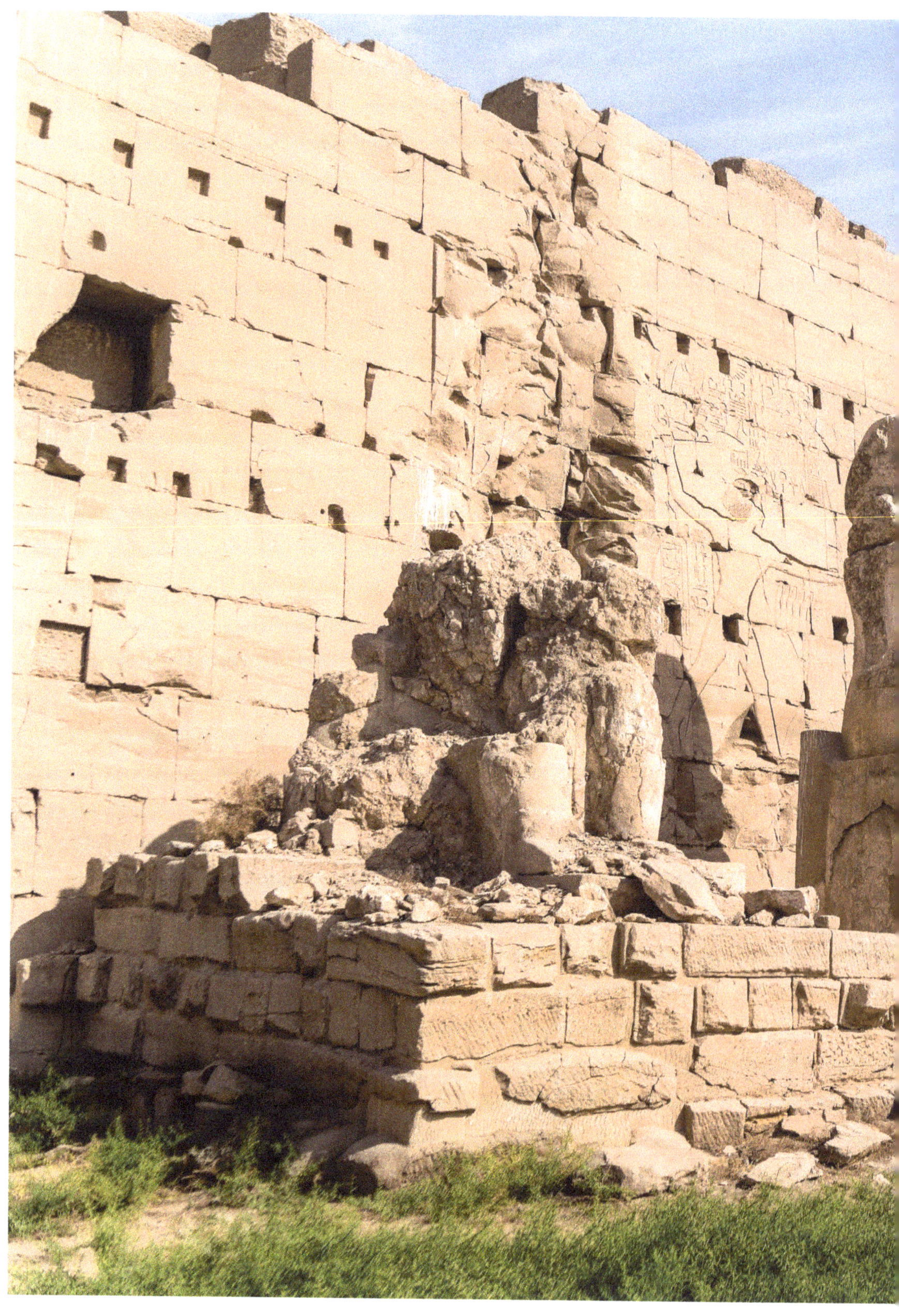

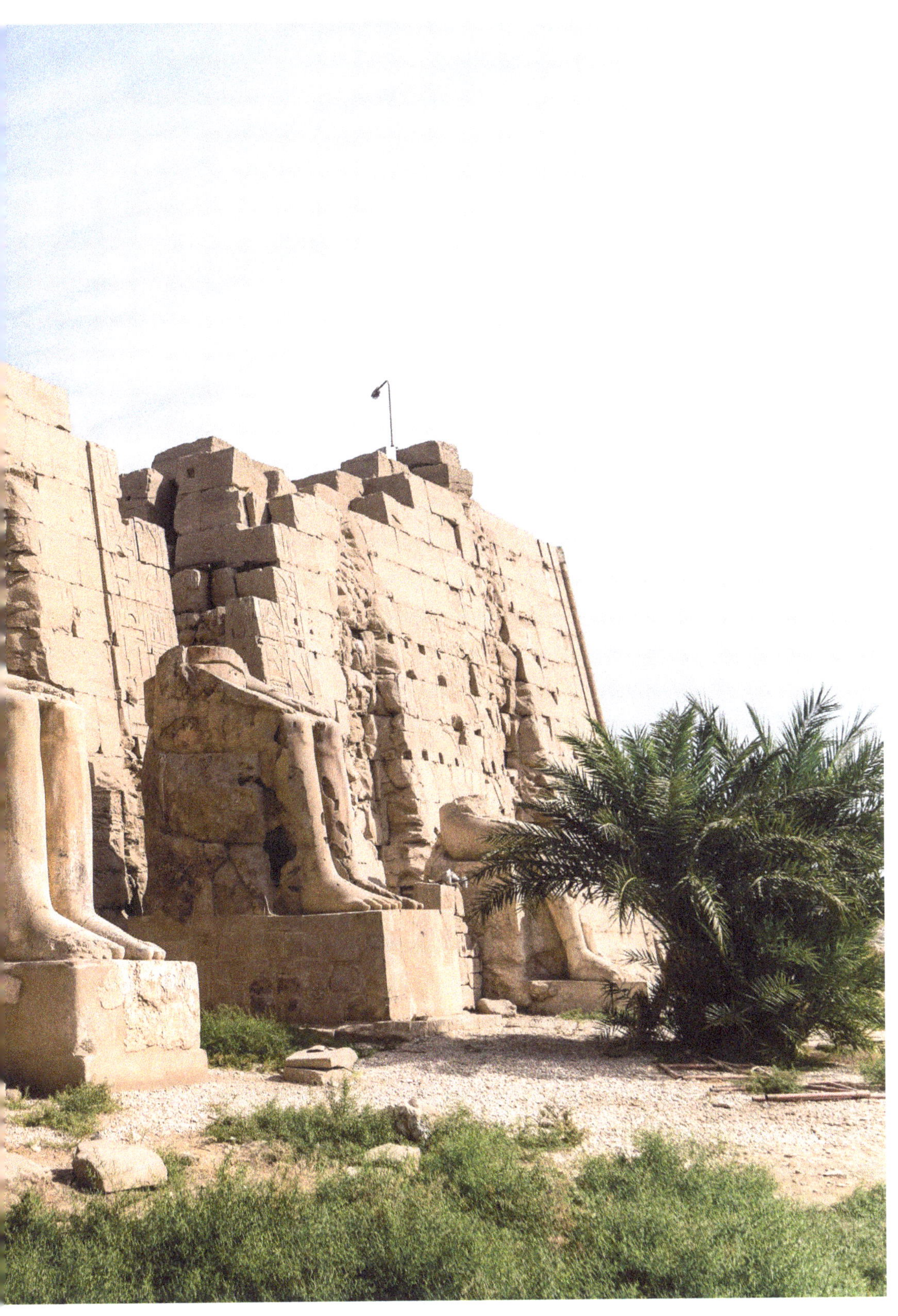

INDEX